COACHING WITH **NLP**

How to be a Master Coach

JOSEPH O'CONNOR
& ANDREA LAGES

element

DEDICATION

Mãezinha
Joseph Desmond O'Connor

Element
An Imprint of HarperCollins*Publishers*
77–85 Fulham Palace Road
Hammersmith, London W6 8JB

The website address is:
www.thorsonselement.com

and *Element* are trademarks of
HarperCollins*Publishers* Limited

Published by Element 2004

A catalogue record for this book
is available from the British Library

ISBN-13   978-0-00-715122-6
ISBN-10   0-00-715122-5

Printed and bound in Great Britain by
Martins the Printers Limited, Berwick upon Tweed

CONTENTS

➡ ACKNOWLEDGEMENTS

Our thanks first to the pioneers of coaching, especially Timothy Gallwey, who have inspired so many people to follow coaching. Thanks to John Grinder and Richard Bandler for creating NLP together. We would like to thank many people who have helped us in the writing of this book, in particular our editor Carole Tonkinson and Elizabeth Hutchins for improving the manuscript with her usual skill and care. We also would like to thank Robin Prior for selflessly helping us to bring this book to reality.

We have learned much from all our students on our training courses, including the postgraduate course we taught in executive coaching. We also think we each have shown great patience and determination in the writing of this book!

Finally, as always, there is some special music we associate with the writing of this book. Thanks to Carlos Santana (as *smooth* as ever) and Gonzaguinha (*O que é O que é?*).

⇒ INTRODUCTION

What are your hopes and dreams?

What is important to you?

Do you have all that you deserve?

What is possible for you?

Imagine a way of exploring these questions with someone to help you realize your best dreams and become the person you always wanted to be. That is coaching.

No wonder coaching is becoming so popular. We live in exciting times. We have fantastic possibilities and want to make the most of them. We feel we deserve happiness; we are willing to invest time, effort and money in improving ourselves and gaining more satisfaction from everything we do. A coach is our guide on the way to being the best we can be.

This is a book about coaching – what it is and how to use it. It is for you if:

you want to be a coach

you are a coach

you want to engage a coach and find out what that entails

you want to coach yourself

you are interested in incorporating coaching into your existing work

This book will help you take your first steps towards becoming a coach. It will add immensely to your skills if you are already a coach. If you are thinking of employing a coach, it will tell you what to expect, and if you want ways to coach yourself, it will help you do that too. If you are engaged in any occupation that aims to help people towards a better life – therapy, counselling, training, mentoring or consultancy – then it will add to your skills, give you new insights and help you become more effective.

The word 'coaching' comes originally from the world of sport, but now coaching is a distinct profession, clearly different from counselling, training, mentoring, therapy and consultancy. What is remarkable is the sheer power and versatility of coaching. Coaching will help you perform a new task, improve your performance in your chosen profession, develop a new skill or solve a problem. In more general terms, many people are turning to coaches to find direction and balance. Life coaches help people to achieve a better life.

Business coaching is becoming increasingly important for three reasons. First, increasingly people are shifting their professional allegiance from their employer to themselves. They invest in their career, which may span many different employers. So companies are realizing that the only way to keep their best people is to invest in them, to develop them and coaching is the best way to do this.

Secondly, coaching key employees is the most focused use of a company's resources because it brings those resources to precisely where they are needed.

Thirdly, the longer-term results of business training are frequently disappointing. On the day, training may be a great success. But if participants go back to the same office the next day, working with the same people who treat them the same way, they will revert to their old behaviour because everything will support that old behaviour. So a great deal of training is wasted money in the long term, because it does not lead to sustainable change. However, with a coach to guide participants after the training, to keep the inspiration alive and help them resist the siren call of 'business as usual', the changes have a much greater chance of sticking. Coaching skills also add immeasurably to the skills of a manager.

In general, coaching offers you the satisfaction of helping people in a remarkably effective way. You can also apply your skills to coach yourself. Coaching is a set of skills and a profession that is wonderfully rewarding and continually expanding.

Coaching with NLP

Neuro-linguistic programming, NLP, is tailor-made for coaching. NLP studies three areas that give it its name:

Neurology	The mind and how we think.
Linguistics	How we use language and how it affects us.
Programming	How we sequence our actions to achieve our goals.

An NLP coach can understand the reality of how a client thinks and can use language very precisely to help that client achieve their goals.

NLP began in the mid-1970s in America with the work of John Grinder, a professor of linguistics, and Richard Bandler, a psychologist. They began by studying excellent communicators, building models of communication skills. The methods could then be taught to others so they too could get the same results. Similarly, we have 'modelled' the patterns of excellent coaches. We can say exactly what works best and what does not. You do not have to reinvent the wheel to be a good coach.

NLP also studies how we structure our subjective experience – how we think about our values and beliefs, how we create our emotional states, how we build our internal world and give it meaning. NLP is the premier psychological field that deals with the internal subjective world from the inside. Coaches need NLP. NLP helps you become a master coach.

However, you do not need to study NLP in its entirety to use it to coach. If you know nothing about NLP, you will find enough of it in this book to use in your coaching. If you are already familiar with NLP, you will see how you can integrate it into your coaching.

What does NLP bring to coaching?

↓ *Speed.* NLP techniques work quickly.

↓ *A pragmatic approach.* If what you are doing does not work, do something else.

↓ *An attitude of fascination.* Every client is unique. How do they do what they do? How can they do it better?

↓ *Simple techniques.* NLP has a number of simple techniques that are tailor-made for coaching.

↓ *An appreciation of how goals, beliefs and values interact.* This is the essence of the coaching process.

↓ *Rapport and trust.* These are prerequisites of a good coaching relationship.

How to Use This Book

This book is divided into four main sections:

↓ The first two chapters set the scene for coaching: what it is and how it works.

↓ Chapters 3 to 8 take you through the structure of coaching and the skills you need from the initial meeting to the end of the coaching relationship. There are also examples of coaching sessions where the skills are used.

↓ Chapter 9 is coaching in action – an example of how some of these tools are used in a real session. Chapter 10 is about coaching yourself.

↓ Finally there is a resource section that includes many of the coaching tools that are referred to in the text, a section on the practicalities of coaching, session lengths, contracts, etc., as well as a glossary of coaching terms and a bibliography.

Taking action is very important in coaching, so there are also some suggestions for tasks for you or your clients at the end of each chapter. These 'Action Steps' can increase your coaching skills and your own self-awareness and happiness. Use those you like and leave any that you do not find useful. Each chapter also has a summary to remind you of the important points.

We have trained coaches from all over the world. Wherever we teach, there is tremendous enthusiasm for coaching and delight and wonder at the remarkable results it brings. We are proud of our international work as coaches, as trainers of coaches and developers of the discipline of coaching. We want to share it with you through this book. We hope you enjoy it and find it useful.

Joseph O'Connor and Andrea Lages
Majorca, 2004

THE DREAM

I had a dream.

Joseph and I are in a big flat space, surrounded by a huge majestic building. The building has many windows that seem to stare down at us. It is almost empty and doesn't seem to have any kind of life, for as we walk our feet send echoes through the high corridors.

It is difficult to see the sky, because the building towers above us. The sky looks more distant than it has ever done.

Every now and again the wind brings distant laughter and we know that despite appearances, somewhere beyond the building people are moving and talking.

We keep walking and walking, and the same things seem to come back to us. 'This is a boring place,' we think, and we wonder if there is any way out of here.

We are there for what seems like a long time and begin to wonder how to get to the top of the building, where we can have a better view. We want to be near the sky. We imagine that somewhere there are stairs to take us to the top, but it looks as though we need to walk through the whole building and search the many floors to find the way. This will take a long, long time and we don't know how to start. We can't find a way inside the building.

The wind begins to blow cold; the sun does not touch us, but threads its fingers into the surrounding shadows.

When night falls and the place becomes dark and frozen, we decide to move.

Suddenly a young woman appears. She is wearing a long dress and has long brown hair. She is carrying an oil lamp in her right hand. The flame from the lamp casts long shadows. These shadows are alive and moving, the other shadows are dead and still.

She walks slowly in our direction, stares at us for a long moment and asks: 'What are you looking for?'

'Can we trust her?' we wonder. 'Can we tell her what we want? Why does she want to know?' We don't even know her.

Why not?

'We want to go to the top of the building.' I point to the exact place where we want to go.

'OK!' she says. 'I will help you, but you need to be very careful. There are dangers.'

PART I

WHAT IS **COACHING?**

CHAPTER 1

FROM IMAGINATION TO REALITY

⇨ ⇨ ⇨ We all dream. While we sleep, our minds shuffle the experiences of the day with their attendant thoughts and emotions like a demented poker player trying to make a winning hand. Those dreams may give us hints, whispers and clues about our lives, where we are now and where we want to go. They dramatize our predicaments and preoccupations – our metaphors become reality in our dreams. But dreams are more than this. When we dream, we use our imagination, we soar beyond the confines of our lives into a wider world where many things are possible and we are not restricted to the cards we have been dealt. We are free to take any wild card and transform our hand. Dreams take us beyond ourselves. Every change in our life starts as a dream – we use our imagination to project ourselves into the best of all futures.

What does coaching have to do with dreams? Coaching is about change, about making changes. A coach is a magician of change who takes the cards you have and help you to play your hand better, or sometimes to change the rules of the game, or find a better game. Changes come from a dream of something better. When we have achieved one dream, we look forward and dream again. There is always a dream beyond the dream.

Ultimately this book is about bringing your dreams into reality. That is what a coach does for you. Coaching engages your imagination and at the same time is immensely practical in the real world. It deals with goals and achievements. It links the world of dreaming with the world of reality.

In 1985, I (Joseph) attended a wonderful music seminar given by a pianist named Eloise Ristad. She worked mainly with concert players who suffered from performance anxiety and had written a great book called *A Soprano on her Head*. The seminar and the book inspired me and as I lay in bed the night after the seminar thinking about my experience, a thought popped into my mind: 'I want to write a book.'

Then the self-talk began in earnest.

'You can't write a book!' came an immediate reply in a rather scornful tone.

'Why not?'

'Er … because you don't know how to.'

'But I can learn. I won't ever know whether I can write a book until I try.'

This little dialogue made clear the difference between belief and ability. What I lacked was the 'know how' to write a book. If I had had a coach then, they would have helped me look at my beliefs, focus on my goal and helped me to realize it. As it was, I acted as my own coach. I set my sights higher than I thought I could. I did not let any limiting beliefs stop me from trying to achieve what I wanted.

You too may be reading this book because you want to be your own coach. You may be interested in coaching in general. You may be interested in becoming a coach, or increasing your coaching skills if you are one already. You may be thinking of hiring a coach. You may want to find out how coaching skills can make you a more effective teacher, trainer or counsellor. You may want to get a new view of your profession and read what someone else thinks about coaching. Whatever your reason, you are going to be closing the gap between dreams and reality for yourself and others.

FIGHTING FOR FREEDOM

A coach is not only a magician of change, but also a freedom fighter.

Freedom faces two ways: freedom from something and freedom to do something. For example, a few years ago, I (Joseph) was working 50 hours a week teaching the guitar. It was satisfying and enjoyable work for the most part, but it was very tiring. It was not the sort of work where I could quietly doze for a few minutes; an instrumental teacher is paid to listen to their students. I loved my work, but I wanted freedom from working so many hours. I wasn't thinking of taking up different work, I just wanted to be able to relax, to have time to gaze into space, read and sleep if I wanted. I did not want to feel so tired. Past a certain threshold, I could not give my work the attention it deserved. Relaxation is just as necessary to being able to work effectively and happily as the time you spend actually working. This is freedom *from*.

The other type of freedom is the freedom *to do something*. Once you are free from one situation, you can do something else. What? In my case it was to write books, to model good writing and prepare and give different training courses.

Coaches work on both types of freedom. They help clients release themselves from unsatisfying or unpleasant circumstances. Then they open out choice and possibilities.

Know your Enemy

If a coach and client are engaged in a fight for freedom, who are the enemies? What stops the change the client wants to make?

Mostly, the enemy is habit. Habitual actions, habitual thinking. Habits that have dug themselves in over time and are hard to move. All habits accomplish something of value, otherwise they would not have become habits in the first place. But times change and our habits may no longer serve our purpose.

Habits are maintained in numerous ways. We arrange our surroundings to support them. Other people expect us to behave in a predictable way and so treat us in a predictable way, reinforcing our habits. Habits are like the cruise control on a car – they are set for a certain speed in a certain direction. Then the driver does not have to pay attention. To change speed and direction, the driver does have to pay attention. Once habits are changed, the new habit will take them in a different direction down a different road.

A coach engages the habits that are holding the client back, sometimes by guerrilla warfare, sometimes by direct assault. Coaching will change the direction of a client's life. Often only one small change at a time. But small changes add up.

Changing Direction

Think of your life as a journey down a road. You don't know where you are heading, but the scenery is pleasant. After a while, you begin to see that it is being recycled. Wait a while and the same thing comes around again. Then you come to a branch in the road. Actually, there have been branches all along the road, but you haven't noticed them. Or if you have, you were comfortable on that road, so you ignored them. Now, however, you have a coach to alert you. You change direction, ever so slightly. You take another road, one that diverges just a little from your original.

The first temptation is to think, 'Huh! Hardly worth doing.' It may be true that the change is only a small one in the short term. But the longer you maintain that change, the further away from your original road you will travel. After a year, you will be in an entirely different country. This will be so even if you never make another change.

The larger the change in direction, the shorter the time it will take to come to new scenery. However, even the slightest change will take you on a different journey if you persist. You just need to keep on that new track, even though the old one may call you back with seductive promises of familiar comforts. 'The devil you know,' it whispers, 'is better than the devil you don't know.' But is there a devil at all on the new road?

What is the role of a coach in this process? A coach does three things:

1　Shows you the track you are on.
2　Points out the choices and helps you take a new road.
3　Helps you persist in that change.

In general, life is a series of small decisions. A big change is often many little changes saved up for the right moment. Each decision we make either keeps us on the same comfortable track or takes us towards what we truly want. Coaching helps us to decide.

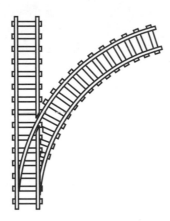

Life is a series of small decisions.

COACHING IN BUSINESS

We have had over a decade of talking about 'learning organizations'. We think there are 'dreaming organizations' too. The dreams exist in the minds of the people who run them. They dream of serving the customers better, of dominating the marketplace with a new product, of the ultimate marketing approach, of the killer application, of new and improved systems to work better, faster and more freely. They dream of being a chameleon organization, one that can change as quickly as its surroundings in a fast-changing market. Coaching can change a business by helping the people in it to dream better dreams and to make those dreams real.

The whole business environment has shifted in the last 20 years. People no longer have jobs for life; they neither seek them nor expect them. They act with 'enlightened selfishness'. The company they work for is no longer as important as their overall career path; they may work in several companies in their working life.

The more people develop themselves, and the more a company develops its people, the more valuable they are to the company. Coaching is one of the most cost-effective and focused ways to do this. It puts the emphasis where it needs to be – on the skills of the people – and leads to quick results.

Life in companies is also a series of small decisions. These small decisions are what keep the company functioning well from day to day and engage the trust and commitment of the workforce. Coaching helps people take high-quality decisions every day.

Ten years ago there was an interesting study about how decisions were taken in a large number of medium-sized European companies. It showed that two-thirds of major decisions were taken in line with declared company strategy. The number dropped to one third when the decisions were of middling importance. However, only one in twenty of the minor everyday decisions were in line with declared company policy. Think about the impression this would have made on the people working there. The major decisions were not very frequent, taken in secret and often not made public for good commercial reasons. So they were mostly invisible. The small day-to-day decisions affected everyone and were obvious and public. Every day people were seeing that the company was not true to its declared policy. Small decisions matter more than the large ones to the people who work in a company.

WHY DO PEOPLE WANT COACHING?

People come for coaching for many different reasons, but there is always some dissonance between their dreams and reality. Sometimes the dissonance is slight. The coaching may be complete in one or two sessions. For example, a manager may want to be able to give more effective feedback to his subordinates. At the moment he either offends people or they do not pay attention. Coach and client work together to understand his intentions and how he is giving feedback now and how he might be misunderstood. Then, with new understanding, he could find different ways to give feedback. He would be given an assignment to give feedback in the new ways and notice the results. The next week he and his coach would discuss what was different and what he had learned.

Other problems may be more complex and take several sessions to resolve, for example a major disappointment in life or a drastic change in situation. A client who is being promoted, for example, might need new skills, and might also need to talk about taking more responsibility and what this means in their life.

What counts as minor inconvenience for one person may be a major disruption for another. When is a problem big or important enough to seek outside help? People have different thresholds. Tolerable limits depend on habit, lifestyle and genetics. Some people need only a slight disturbance to feel uncomfortable whereas others will tolerate a great deal before they act to remedy a situation.

There is a joke about two frogs. One is hopping along at the bottom of a deep rut made by a tractor. The other sees him there and shouts down, 'Hey! What are you doing down there? It's much better up here; there is more food.'

The other frog looks up. 'I can't get out.'

'Let me help you,' says the second frog.

'No. Leave me alone. I'm OK. There is plenty of food down here for me.'

'OK,' says the second frog. 'But there is much more space up here to explore and move around.'

'I've got all the space I need down here.'

'But what about meeting other frogs?'

'They come down here sometimes, otherwise I can shout to my friends up there.'

The second frog heaves the frog equivalent of a sigh and hops on.

The next day, he is surprised to see the first frog hopping up beside him.

'Hey!' he shouts. 'I thought you were staying down in that rut. What happened?'

'There was a truck coming.'

For some people it takes the equivalent of a truck to move them. Other people may be reasonably satisfied and successful, but believe that 'you do not have to be sick to get better'. These people will engage a coach to explore how they can be happier and even more effective. They want to be the best they can be, and they want their best to get better all the time.

Whatever the situation, a client may ask the coach explicitly or implicitly to put their life back to how it was before the disruption. In other words, once the truck has passed, then the rut may look attractive again. The coach must avoid this temptation at all costs, otherwise there will be trouble. First, it is impossible. You cannot turn the clock back. Secondly, even if you could, the client would be open to exactly the same problem again. Trying to put them back where they were leads to a coaching equivalent of Groundhog Day, with the same problem endlessly recurring. Coaching helps people to take a new direction, to take steps towards happiness, not to run comfortably on the same spot.

HAPPINESS

Coaching is a game for high stakes: happiness. People come to be coached because they want to be happy, or happier. They want a satisfying life filled with good experiences. They want good relationships, a job they enjoy and are proud of, where they can use their talents and make money. They want to experience life's pleasures to the full. They want to see their good dreams come true and feel they are living their highest values. They want to be liked by many, loved by some and respected by all.

Business coaching plays for equally high stakes, maybe the very survival of the business. A thriving business is profitable, good to work in, achieves its goals and operates according to its core values. It is respected in the marketplace. For a business to thrive and be successful, people need to be happy in their work and good at what they do.

Happiness is not a prescription you can go and have filled by a happiness chemist. It's not something you possess, but something you *are*. Everybody has a different idea of what will make them happy and a coach cannot know in advance what will make a client happy. Sometimes the client does not know either.

There is some interesting research that suggests that about two-thirds of us do not know how to be happy. In 1957, there was a research project in the United States of America asking a large number of people whether they were happy with what they had in life. About one third said yes. In 1992, when the same study was repeated, the same percentage said yes, despite the fact that the standard of living had increased considerably. What does this mean? It means that about one third of the people know the secret of being happy: that it comes from the inside. It does not depend on what you have, but what you are and what you experience. Being happy is in the small things of life, that series of small decisions, each one making you happier. Happiness is in the everyday details of life.

Many people think of pursuing happiness. When they have that next possession, feeling or person, then they will be happy. This is a mirage. The very language betrays it. If you are pursuing happiness, you have put it ahead of you. As long as you continue to pursue it, it will stay tantalizingly out of reach. You cannot pursue something you have. You can only be happy *right now*.

Many people also think that to be happy is somehow selfish, that there is only so much happiness to go around and if they are happy then inevitably someone will have to pay. Yet perhaps being happy is good for everyone. And the only person's happiness you can deal with is your own.

How happy are you? Coaching is about increasing self-awareness – finding out where you are and looking for ways to move forward. One way to do this is through self-observation exercises. We are going to offer you a number of such exercises throughout this book.

Take a few moments to think about the next questions. Don't skip over them to get on to the next page. They play for high stakes. Some may appear simple, but often coaching is asking simple questions. The quality of a question is not judged by its complexity, but by the complexity of thinking that it provokes.

Write down your answers, but don't take a long time unless you really want to. If you put down what comes into your head immediately, it will be nearer the truth.

Happiness: Self-observation

What does being happy mean to you?
Think of a time when you were happy. What was it like?

TRUST

Trust is crucial in the coaching relationship. But why trust a coach? Why trust anybody? What has to happen for you to trust?

Trust, like happiness, is an abstraction. It's not an object you can possess, but a relationship created between people. The word comes from the Old Norse *traustr*, meaning 'strong'. We trust in what we think is true. When we trust someone we believe them to be strong, we can metaphorically lean on them without fear that they will collapse.

Trust takes time. It is very rare that one person will trust another immediately unless there is an overwhelmingly powerful reason. When Arnold Schwarzenegger extends his arm to Sarah Connor in the film *Terminator 2*, she has to trust him, at least in that context, or die. More usually trust is built over time, with repeated testing in different circumstances.

The word 'truth' comes from the same root as trust, but trust is not about objective truth. Suppose one person tells you it is sunny outside, another that it is raining. The question of trust is not about the weather, but whether you can believe the person. If you cannot look outside, you have to decide on the basis of which person is the more trustworthy. We need trust when we cannot see what is happening for ourselves.

How is trust built between coach and client? First, trust comes from knowing yourself. Unless you know yourself, your boundaries, goals and values, you may trust too soon, because you want to believe the other person. Or you may trust too readily because you ask for too little from the other person for them to be trustworthy. In these cases, you may be exploited.

On the other hand, you may have very high standards and demand impossible feats of bravery and achievement before you trust anyone. In this case, you may become lonely and emotionally isolated.

Trust: Self-observation

Think of someone you trust.
> **How did you decide you trusted them?**
> **What did they do or not do?**
> **What evidence did you want before you trusted them?**
> **How long did it take before you trusted them?**

Now think of someone you do not trust.
> **How did you decide you did not trust them?**
> **What did they do or not do?**
> **How long did it take before you decided they were not trustworthy?**

We often say that trust has to be 'earned'. However, trust is not a matter of accounting, adding up a person's positives and subtracting their negatives to see if the equation balances. Trust is more flexible. It is not an all-or-nothing quality. Rather than think about whether a person is trustworthy in the abstract, it is more useful to consider how far you trust a person and in what context. You might trust a friend completely with your money, but not with your romantic partner. I (Andrea) once had a friend who was always there for me when I needed her; I felt I could trust her in almost everything – except when my boyfriend was around. Then she was more interested in being available to him.

We usually judge trust by two criteria. The first is sincerity, or subjective truthfulness. We have to judge this by a person's behaviour. Does their behaviour match an inner depth, an inner truthfulness to themselves and others? Are they sincere? Do they follow through on their promises? Are their words and actions consistent with each other, and are they consistent when they are speaking to different people?

The second aspect of trust is competence. A person may be sincere, but are they capable of carrying out what they promise?

A coach needs to be sincere *and* competent to be trustworthy. They also need to be a model for the qualities they seek to bring out in the client.

This chapter is about waking up from dreams and taking action. Coaching is the way to do this. How it can be applied in life and work is the focus of the next chapter.

SUMMARY

Our dreams shape our goals and our goals shape our life.
A coach helps us achieve our goals.

A coach fights with the client for freedom:
    freedom from circumstances that the client does not want
    freedom to choose what they want
The enemies of freedom are the habits that keep us comfortable the way we are.
Our surroundings, friends and family tend to reinforce our habits.
A series of small decisions can change our lives.

A coach will:
    show you the track you are on
    point out where you can change
    support the change

Coaching helps business by helping the people who run it.
Coaching is one of the most cost-effective and focused ways to develop people in business.

People engage a coach for different reasons, usually because something has broken down in their life. The coach will help them to resolve this and move on, not put them back where they were before.
Some people come for coaching because although they are happy, they want to be happier.

Coaching is about helping people be happy.
Everyone wants to be happy but many people do not know how.
An important part of coaching is to make the client more self-aware.

A client needs to trust the coach.
Trust is built over time.
A coach must be sincere and competent to be trustworthy.

ACTION STEPS

If you want to understand, act. Here are some ways to explore the ideas in this chapter. You can also use them as tasks for your client and yourself if you wish.

1   Choose a photograph that you really like of yourself between the ages of 5 and 12.

    Remember the good things you knew that you were able to do in life, for example, playing, doing jigsaw puzzles, running, putting together model airplanes, writing essays. Visualize yourself doing these things.

    Ask yourself now, 'What did those things get for me and how can I bring more of that into my life?'

2   Start to write for 10 minutes every morning; not serious writing, just a 'brain dump'. You do not have to say anything meaningful, just write one page on whatever you want. Do it longhand, because your hand connects your brain directly with the paper. It is the equivalent of thinking out loud, of trying out thoughts for size. The few minutes this takes can clear your mind for the day and lead to some great insights. Buy yourself a special notebook. Make it a

habit. Do it every day for at least three months. It will repay you a thousandfold.

3   Watch the film *Shallow Hal* on video.
    What do you think makes Hal happy?
    What makes the Gwyneth Paltrow character happy?

4   Many people think that you need a lot of money to live 'like a millionaire', but you do not. You do not need 20 of something to be happy, just one very good one that you like. Think of some of great pleasures:
    sleeping
    eating
    leisure
    clothes
and make sure you have the best you can afford – a good mattress to sleep on, for example. It need not be expensive. Good food does not have to be expensive. You are mostly paying for the surroundings in expensive restaurants. Take up a leisure pursuit that you really enjoy. Beautiful comfortable clothes do not need to be expensive. What you pay for is often the little tag that shows the brand. Buy the best you can. You may be more comfortable and better dressed than many millionaires.

5   Think of a problem that you have at the moment that you are not doing anything about yet.

    Now think of a problem that you are taking 'real action' to solve. What is important about that problem?

    What does this tell you about your thresholds for dealing with problems?

6   Whenever you have a decision to make, ask yourself, 'Will this lead to more or less happiness?'

 COACHING IN LIFE AND WORK

 This chapter looks at coaching from the outside – definitions and methods – and how it can be applied. What is coaching? How is it different from other methods?

This last is a very important question. Coaching has been confused with training and counselling in particular, and it is essential to make the distinction.

Coaching is a partnership in which the coach helps the client to achieve their personal best and to produce the results they want in their personal and professional lives. The intention of coaching is similar to that of other helping professions: helping a person change in the way they wish and supporting them in becoming the best they can be.

DIFFERENT TYPES OF COACHING

There are different sorts of coaching, but the skills involved are the same, only applied in different areas. A coach may specialize, but there is often considerable overlap, for example between life coaching and business coaching. A life coach cannot work without looking at the client's job, for example, and a business coach cannot do the client justice unless they help them fit their work into their life.

Life Coaching

A life coach deals with the client's life in all its dimensions – personal and professional life, health and relationships. There will always be an immediate issue, but this will broaden out to touch on many aspects of the client's life, for example diet, exercise, relationships with partner and children, and satisfaction with work, career, retirement and living conditions.

Executive Coaching

Executive coaches specialize in coaching executives. They deal with people who have authority and power in an organization. Executive coaches are familiar with this world and fit into it. They may be directors themselves who have trained in coaching and therefore know about the sort of pressures that top executives are under and the sort of decisions they have to make.

A top executive occupies a lonely position. They are supposed to have answers, people come to them for guidance and it is not easy for them to talk over the pressures and difficulties of their work with a sympathetic and capable person. There is often no one in the organization that they can really talk to about their hopes and dreams, doubts and fears. An executive coach fulfils this very important role.

A top executive who works better has a huge positive effect on a company. It could mean millions of pounds of extra profit. The return on executive coaching can be enormous.

Business Coaching

Executive coaching is the top end of business coaching. Business coaches coach people in their work on professional issues. They often work with managers inside a company and may coach teams. For example, an executive may have difficulty with other executives and need coaching, or a director may need clarity about their vision and values and the business mission and purpose, or teams may have coaching to make them more effective.

Coaching concentrates on individuals, not business systems, but coaching will impact and improve the results of a business indirectly.

Business coaching is also the best follow-up to any type of consultancy or training. Without coaching, training and consultancy are often a waste of money, as the inertia of the system will take it back to where it was before. Resistance to change is not bad, it is inevitable. A business has stability, otherwise it would collapse. Therefore it resists change – any sort of change, including the change that you want.

Often business coaching shades into life coaching because no one can separate their work from the rest of their life. Often managers do not perform well because something in their personal life is worrying them, for example their relationship with their partner.

The Manager as Coach

Can a person be a manager and a coach at the same time? This is an important question. As the popularity of coaching grows, many businesses try to combine the two roles by training managers in coaching, or worse, expecting the manager to be able to coach with no training at all.

A manager can certainly do informal coaching, however it is very difficult for a manager to substitute for a trained external coach for four reasons:

1   The manager will see their 'client' every day, and this makes it more difficult to be objective.
2   The manager is busy enough without adding an extra task to their workday.
3   Their main responsibility is to the business, not to the client, and this makes confidentiality a tricky issue.
4   The manager may be responsible for appraising the same individual they are coaching and this leads to problems. How easy is it for the 'client' to confess to their manager that they do not like their work or they think that they are being badly managed? Whatever the reality, the client will have to hold back on significant feelings and experiences about their work.

So, while the manager as coach may work within well-defined boundaries, such as improving a skill in the short term, an external coach will give better results overall.

Career Coaching

A career coach specializes in coaching people who want to find a job, change career, or get back into the job market after a break from work. This is an increasingly important area. In the Western world, there are more people than jobs for two reasons. First, more qualified people are coming on the job market. Secondly, many jobs have been lost due to advancing technology. One computer can do the job that was previously done by half a dozen people. Many people are taking early retirement and are living longer, so there are thousands of people who would like to work but find it hard to do so. From 2003 in the UK, changes in the pension structure will mean that most people will work until the age of 70. This means that top jobs will be occupied longer and this will have a knock-on effect. It is already nearly impossible for anyone over 50 years of age to get a new salaried job.

Career coaches often work together with an outplacement agency. However, career planning must also come into business and life coaching, so this is not an isolated area.

Sports Coaching

Here is where the concept of coaching began. Coaching has traditionally been associated with sport and all serious athletes now have a coach, usually a senior player who has been successful in their time, though not necessarily at the highest level. But why do only *top* athletes have a coach? Maybe they are at the top *because* they have a coach. Why shouldn't every athlete who is serious about their game have a coach?

All types of coaching are fascinating and share the same patterns – establishing goals and values and building skills for the future. Whatever area you have chosen to specialize in, you will be taking your client beyond their perceived limits.

Coaching focuses on understanding the present and designing the future, not 'fixing' or understanding the past. Coaching is usually one to one rather than one to many, although team coaching is very effective too. The coach is not the expert, may not have detailed knowledge of the client's business and asks questions rather than gives answers. Add these differences together and they give a characteristic approach that is different from all others. The differences between coaching and other approaches such as training and mentoring are summarized on page 169 in the Resources to Chapter 2.

THE INNER GAME

Although in the last few years coaching has become applicable to every area of life, it still carries the imprint of its sporting beginnings – the emphasis is on action, accomplishment, excellence, being the best and the importance of measurable results.

In 1974 Timothy Gallwey's highly influential book, *The Inner Game of Tennis* was published. If coaching can be traced back to any one book, this is it. Although Gallwey was a tennis coach, he applied ideas from sports coaching in a much wider way so they became universally relevant. He concentrated on the inner game – the battle each athlete has with their own mental limitations.

An athlete who is competing has two opponents. One is their outer opponent on the track, court or ring. The other is the inner opponent: their own limitations. You win the inner game first in order to win the outer game. Often the inner opponent is the tougher of the two. Gallwey identified the inner opponent as the part that thinks too much, overanalyses and 'tries' hard. The trying gets in the way of the doing. He put the emphasis on awareness, knowing what you are really doing (not what you should be doing), so you can change it. These principles apply in every type of coaching.

Coaching answers the basic question 'How can I be better?' This is the same question that began NLP. There are exceptional people in every walk of life. What is the difference between the exceptional people and the average? NLP looked for the answer to this question by modelling the exceptional people to find out how they did what they did so well. How did they think? How did they use their body? What were their goals, their values and their beliefs about themselves and about others? How did they use language? Out of these pieces NLP built models that work. In other words, if you act as the model acts, you will get the same class of results that the model gets: excellent results.

The Three Supports of Coaching

Beliefs, values and goals provide the support for coaching, much like the three legs of a stool.

1 Coaching focuses on what you want – your goal – and how to achieve it.
2 Coaching encourages you to know your values and live them in achieving your goals.
3 Coaching challenges limiting beliefs and reinforces positive ones by giving tasks that provide feedback.

Building Skills

Coaching, like NLP, builds skill. It implements four of the core NLP presuppositions:

1 *Everyone has the resources they need or can acquire them.* A coach always treats the client as resourceful. The coach does not have the answer, the client does. The coach makes the client aware of their situation, works with them on their goals and values, points out where they can make choices, fights habits that are holding them back and supports them in the changes they make.
2 *People make the best choice they can at the time.* We are all doing our best right now. When we know more and have more choices, our best will take us further towards where we want to go. We are often like a runner running hard and well, but down the wrong track. Our running is great; our direction is off the mark.
3 *Human behaviour is purposeful.* We are all driven by goals and values – what we want and why we want it. These are what lead to change.
4 *If you want to understand, act!* The last and in some ways the most important, because without it the rest are just nice ideas. There are many people who understand why they are stuck, but without action they cannot understand how to change. Any coaching that does not result in new behaviour is futile.

However, unlike NLP, coaching is not about applying a set of tools. Coaching is more a stance, a relationship based on those ideas. The outcome of coaching is long-term excellence and the ability for the client to move forward on their own – to be self-generative. Like any good teacher, a good coach must always be working to become redundant, not indispensable.

SUMMARY

There are five main areas of specialization for coaches:
↓ *business coaching*
↓ *executive coaching*
↓ *career coaching*
↓ *life coaching*
↓ *sports coaching*
Coaching began in sports, but is now applicable to every area of life.
Coaching answers the basic question: 'How can I be better?'

The three areas of coaching are:
1 *Goals: focusing on what you want and how to achieve it.*
2 *Values: knowing what is important to you and living your values in achieving your goals.*
3 *Beliefs: challenging limiting beliefs by giving tasks that provide feedback.*
4 *Coaching implements four of the core NLP presuppositions:*
   1 *Everyone has the resources they need or can acquire them.*
   2 *People make the best choice they can at the time.*
   3 *Human behaviour is purposeful.*
   4 *If you want to understand, act!*

Coaching shares some aspects of counselling, therapy, training, teaching, consultancy and mentoring. It also has a characteristic approach that is different from all of these. Coaching is generative, focuses on the present and future, and understands through taking action.

ACTION STEPS

If you want to understand, act. Here are some ways to explore the ideas in this chapter. You can also use them as tasks for your client and yourself if you wish.

1 What skill in your life would you most like to improve?
   How would you decide when you were good enough?

2 Design your perfect work.
   What work do you really enjoy so much that it does not seem like work?
   How would you like to work?
   Where would you like to work? Design your perfect work environment.
   When would you like to work? Design your perfect working day.
   What is the first action step you can take that would bring you closer to this reality?
   Do it.

3 What are you most grateful for in your life?
   How can you have more of this?
   Do one thing today that will bring you more of this.

⟶ THE DREAM CONTINUES...

It seems that the strange woman knows this place very well... We don't yet know exactly what she is doing here, but maybe she can help us. She has said that we need to be careful in this area and we wonder, 'Careful about what?' We have spent ages exploring the place and we haven't seen any dangers at all. Everything has looked boring...
Then we realize that we have been walking in circles!

The strange woman said that the dangers were in the places where you don't go. Maybe she meant the dangers were in the areas where we haven't been before. So there are many other things to see. We have the feeling that there is something strange just beyond our vision, like a movement you see out of the corner of your eye. Sometimes we also can hear laughter on the wind, but it is impossible to know where it is coming from... Maybe this is the answer.

Suddenly we see a big wooden double door. Wow! We haven't seen that door before, yet it has been there all the time! It is very close, how could we have missed it? It looks like the door of a big old mansion; it has beautiful intricate carvings on both sides that seem to shift as we look at them.

We walk towards the door and see a lift. It is completely packed with people and we don't think there is enough space for us, but this does not seem to worry our mysterious companion.

The lift door slides shut. It's gone.

We wonder what to do and then we see the lady opening the door of another lift.

This new lift is completely empty, very different from the first one ... and it doesn't look so new either. The doors have the same intricate pattern as the big doors outside, beautiful but a little bizarre for a lift.

The woman opens the door and beckons us inside. We stay where we are, not knowing exactly what to do. She asks: 'Do you *really* want to go to the top?' and starts closing the door…

'Yes, but…'

She shakes her head in an understanding sort of way and whispers: 'If you do, mind the gap.'

We are inside. The floor of the lift is not strong; it is swaying as if we were standing in a hammock. Maybe this is why everyone took the first lift…

One side of the lift is transparent; we can see the building moving downwards as we rise. The lift sways like a demented pendulum; the movement is so strong that we can hardly stand. Everything is swaying except for the flame of the woman's lamp. That stays completely steady. Somehow, we are not surprised.

We don't have long to think about it in any case, because just when we thought that the lift was coming to a stop, another shake almost throws us out.

We stay quiet; we are afraid. We look at the woman and she seems to be enjoying the ride. It all seems quite normal to her. Is she crazy?

We've left the ground, but will we reach the top?

We don't know, but there is no way back.

The lift goes up a long way; it seems to cling to the side of the building like an insect. We remember just how big the building is. Why did we start?

Then the lift stops with a shudder and the door opens. We fall out with relief. That was not an easy journey, but now are we nearer to where we want to be?

We look around and the view is amazing. There are many more things around us than we realized. The building is more like a city. From up here we can see so much more life; there are people and flowers everywhere. We can see, far below, the places where we were walking, and many places we never noticed, even when we were in the middle of them. We can see the big circles we were walking in.

A huge gothic cathedral catches our attention. Now that would be interesting to visit.

The woman comes over to join us. Her eyes move gently over the view.

Behind us is the majestic cathedral. We decide to go and look at that.

PART 2

THE ART OF **COACHING**

CHAPTER 3

GOALS AND VALUES

How satisfied are you with your life at the moment? We tend to get used to what we have. We keep doing the same old things that we have always done and that have always worked. Our lives may be comfortable, but still there may be a nagging feeling: do I have everything I deserve right now?

The beauty and danger of modern life is that you need to keep moving in your own direction, otherwise people will move you in theirs. If you don't know what you want, it is easy to find someone who will tell you what *they* want you to do and will try to make you do it. If that suits you, maybe this is the time to stop reading this book. If you want something else out of life, if you want to have everything that you deserve, carry on reading… Do you have everything you deserve right now?

Life is a series of small decisions. Each one seems inconsequential, yet together they add up. Each is important. Whole lives can be changed because of an apparently small decision. Everything we do, every small decision, has some purpose, and taking charge of your life means having your own purpose and setting your own goals, not letting others set them for you. All successful people set goals. Goals are dreams with legs – they go somewhere!

When I (Andrea) first became interested in goals, I wondered if they really worked in real life or whether they were just a nice idea. I had read a lot about how people could achieve amazing things by working with goals and doing something different from what they would normally do. One day I decided to test this idea. The worst that could happen would be that nothing would change!

I had been working hard for years, yet I was not enjoying my life. Had I been working hard for something I did not want? This was definitely *not* the life that I had dreamed about.

I took an important step forward: I started to write down my goals. I started to put in place the first brick to build my life today. I wanted to make a difference.

When I started to work seriously with goals, a lot of things happened… Before this, all my professional life had been dedicated to the arts, especially theatre. I had spent years living inside theatres and cinema studios, working day and night, and it had been fascinating. It was a wonderful life, nevertheless I was convinced that I needed to do something else if I was to be truly fulfilled. It is not easy to start on a new way, with no guarantee of getting what you want at the end. I was afraid. It is normal to feel afraid of the unknown. Fear, however, can be very positive if you can direct the energy it contains. Fear drives us forward, it can be motivating when it is not paralysing. Fear is a survival instinct, so it has a role in life, but it often keeps us in the same safe place. I respected my fear and was grateful for it.

When we have enough support to go for our goals (this support can be belief in the future and in our possibilities), we can transcend our fear. We then encounter a transition time, when we have left the safety of where we are, but have not yet arrived at where we want to be. This time can be your best friend (it makes you more prepared for the goal), or your worst enemy (it makes you stop believing that your goal is possible just because you are not there *yet*). When I decided to leave the world of cinema to become an NLP trainer, I was not prepared. I had read many books on the subject, but that was all. So, although I was impatient, the time of transition was my best friend, because it gave me the opportunity to prepare for my goal.

This was all some years ago. Now I am sitting in a beautiful villa in Majorca writing this book about NLP and coaching together with a very special person with whom I share the most beautiful moments and realizations in my life. Our relationship is based in friendship, love and complete trust – just what I always wanted. We spend much of our time travelling, giving coaching and NLP courses, and we are very happy. I remember that many times in my life I almost stopped believing that was possible. I am glad I kept believing my goals were possible through every step of the journey.

Now I smile as I think back to the words I wrote on that piece of paper many years ago. Those words – my goals – were the most powerful words I have ever written.

EXPLORING THE PRESENT AND DESIGNING THE FUTURE

A goal is a dream with legs. What does this mean?

Goals are what drive us forward. They are what we want. Why do we even get out of bed in the morning? Because we want something. It may be trivial, like breakfast; it may be great, like improving someone's life through worthwhile work. Goals are the bedrock of coaching. Coaching helps clients to articulate what they want, to dream good dreams, to give those dreams legs and to run with them.

We are always moving towards something. We are moving from a present state to a desired state. The moment we are dissatisfied with what we have, we are on a journey towards something better. What distinguishes one person from another is what they want. Some people have every material comfort, yet are dissatisfied. Others live very simply, yet may be very satisfied. Our goals are just as unique to us as our fingerprints.

The opposite of goal-setting is problem-thinking. This focuses on what is wrong. Many people get lost in a labyrinth of problems, finding out the history, cost and consequences of problems as well as who is to blame. Goal-setting shifts the question from 'What's wrong?' to 'What do I want?' This takes you forward in a structured way.

A coach helps a client to explore the present and design the future. They take the client from where they are to where they want to be by giving them more choice and more resources for their journey.

This involves two different types of goal:

↓ *The outcome goal*: your destination, where you are heading.
↓ *The process goal*: your journey, how you are going to get there. When you make a plan to achieve your outcome goal, this will involve a number of smaller goals and these will make up your journey.

Distinguishing these two very different aspects of goal-setting is crucial. Much advice about goals mixes them together.

THE SEVEN GOLDEN RULES OF GOALS

When you set a goal, it must be worthwhile. It must express your values, otherwise why do it at all? There are seven golden rules of goals that are immensely useful in establishing your own goals and also helping others with their goals. These rules apply to professional and personal goals as well as goals for a company.

1. Goals are expressed in the positive.

Every outcome goal should be expressed in the positive – it should be what you want, not what you don't want or want to avoid. Many clients see what is wrong with their life and want to move away from it. They will tell you exactly what they do not want. But setting a negative goal is like going shopping with a list of things that you do not want to buy.

The power of goal-setting is that it fixes your attention and focuses your thoughts. If you set a negative goal, then it fixes your attention on what you do not want. So, for example, if you set out not to lose money, then 'losing money' will preoccupy your thoughts. If you set a goal to give up smoking, then your attention will be fixed on smoking. Much better to think about what you want instead – in these cases, making money, better health and relaxation.

This golden rule only applies to the *outcome goal* – in other words, to your destination. A destination must be positive; it is something you move towards. However, the process goal – how you get there – may well have some negatives. In fact getting the goal might involve giving up something. This is something we will deal with when we come to drawing up an action plan (*pages 39–42*).

> **Key questions to ask the client for the first golden rule:**
> ↓   **'What do you want?'**
> ↓   **'What do you want instead?'**
> ↓   **'What would you rather have?'**

2. Make the goal specific.

Make your outcome goal, that is your destination, as specific as possible. For some goals this is easy, for example a new computer, a new car, a new house. For abstract or intangible goals, it is more difficult. It is hard to be specific about a better relationship or wanting more confidence. For these abstract goals, be specific about the evidence that will let you know you have them. For example, if the goal is to have more confidence, you can say that means you will be able to make an after-dinner speech of 10 minutes without breaking out in a cold sweat and lying awake tossing and turning the night before. The speech would have to be recognized as reasonable by at least two people present who will swear to give truthful feedback.

For objective outcomes – for example, 'I want a new car', where the outcome is a sensory specific, describable object – make the outcome specific, but between certain appropriate boundaries. Do not be a perfectionist. A perfectionist is not only too specific, but will not settle for anything less.

A coach starts with a client's long-term goals, and in long-term goals it is not possible to be very specific. It is not possible to pin down the future like a butterfly in a glass case. The closer the goals, the more specific you can be. You can say *when, where and with whom* you will achieve them.

In abstract outcomes – for example, 'I want more confidence', where confidence is an abstract quality – do not try to specify the outcome, instead specify what you want to see, hear and feel – the evidence that will let you know that you have it.

One thing that should *always* be specified is the time scale:

↓　How long will this goal take?
↓　When do you want the goal?
↓　How long is needed to achieve it?

This applies to both the journey and the destination. How long the journey takes gives you the time you will reach your destination.

> **Key questions:**
> ↓　**'What exactly do you want?'**
> ↓　**'Can you describe that more precisely?'**
> ↓　**'What exactly will you see and hear when you get that?'**
> ↓　**'How long will that take?'**
> ↓　**'When do you want to achieve that goal?'**

3. Decide how you will get evidence and feedback for achievement.

For the outcome goal, it is important to set the evidence that will tell you that you have achieved it. When you see, hear and feel X, Y and Z, then you have your outcome.

For the process goal, the journey, what will guide you is feedback. Feedback will show you whether you are on track for your destination. Feedback for a salesperson, for example, is the quality of rapport that they achieve with a customer, the small buying signals they show in response to the benefits of the product. A good salesperson is closing throughout the sale and they do that by tracking customer feedback from their body language, voice tone and words.

You can easily miss the goal entirely if you don't pay attention to the feedback you are getting. This applies especially to long-term goals. Imagine an aeroplane taking off from São Paulo to fly to Honolulu. The pilot plots the course; Honolulu is the destination. However, the pilot does not just let the plane fly itself after take-off. He constantly monitors the flying conditions, the height of the aircraft, the amount of other air traffic, all the safety equipment and of course the direction, to make sure the plane is still on track. He knows it was on track when they left São Paulo, but the journey needs constant attention. It is important even if there are no unexpected emergencies; in fact the constant monitoring is part of ensuring that there *are* no unexpected emergencies. If aeroplanes do this with all their failsafe computer equipment, how much more important it must be in the uncertainties and vagaries of human communication.

So when you are helping a client to set their goals you need to ask them several questions to help them think about feedback:

↓   'How will you measure your progress?'

There are two main ways, although most goals will have elements of both methods:

1   *Relative to yourself.* You measure your own performance once and then measure again later and notice how much you have improved.
2   *Relative to another person.* For example, suppose you want to come top of the sales team next month. In order to do this, you need not necessarily do any better than you are doing at the moment, but others have to do worse.

↓   'How often will you measure your progress?'

If we go back to our flight to Honolulu, the pilot is constantly making sure the aeroplane is on track. It would be foolish to wait a long time between measurements. At 500 miles per hour, an aircraft can go a long way off course in half an hour. In fact it is never precisely on course. Sometimes it is off to the right, sometimes off to the left. The pilot has to correct constantly, otherwise the plane will have travelled a long way in the wrong direction and the correction will be more difficult and take longer. The same principles apply to goals. We always need to be looking for feedback to ensure we are on track for our goals.

If we have benchmarks on the road, then we can keep ourselves on track. These benchmarks can be our guide; their absence can be our ruin. In very cold countries, people put tall sticks on both sides of the roads about 10 yards apart. They look strange in the summer, sticking up forlornly, but when snow has covered road and field alike they show you are on the road. Without them, you could be driving in the middle of a field or over the edge of a mountain.

> **Key questions:**
> ↓ 'How will you know that you have achieved your goal?'
> ↓ 'What milestones will you set up along the way?'
> ↓ 'How will you know that you are on track for this goal?'
> ↓ 'How often will you check that you are on track?'

4. Marshall your resources.

You need resources on the *journey*. (You do not need them for the destination.) Resources can be:

↓ *Objects*: Books you have read, equipment and technology, audiotapes and videotapes with information you need.

↓ *People*: Family, friends, colleagues, other contacts that you have, maybe from a long time ago.

↓ *Time*: Do you have enough time to dedicate to the achievement of the goal? If not, how can you create it? How will you deal with long delays?

↓ *Role models*: Do you know anyone who has already succeeded in obtaining that goal? What can you learn from them? Has someone written about what they did to achieve the goal? Is there a fictional character in a book, play or film that you can use as a model?

↓ *Personal qualities*: What qualities (skills and capabilities) do you have or need to develop to achieve your outcome?

The goal may seem a large one and very far away and the journey may seem long and arduous, but a small resource in just the right place can make a difference. Small push, big effect. This is leverage rather than brute force. Leverage is the principle of getting the most effect for the smallest effort, and it can mean stopping doing things just as much as doing them. Think of leverage when you use resources.

> **Key questions:**
> ↓ 'What resources will you need to achieve that goal?'
> ↓ 'What resources do you have already?'
> ↓ 'Where will you find the resources you need?'

5. Be proactive.

This principle again applies to the *journey*, not the destination. To reach your goal, *you* must take action, not someone else. You must feel the cause of your life, not the effect. Many clients come to coaching feeling that they are always being pushed around, that they are always responding to what other people are doing, rather than doing anything for themselves. The first step for them is to set their goals and here this rule is particularly important.

There are two ways of talking about what we do and the words reflect how we think about it. The first is what is called 'the active voice'. This means *you* are the subject of the verb, *you* do something, for example 'I did this' or 'I set the goals' or 'I gave the presentation.'

The second way of talking is 'the passive voice'. This puts the emphasis on *what* was done and wipes out *who* did it, for example 'The goals were set', 'The presentation went OK.' Nowhere does it say *who* did these things. Sometimes clients use the passive voice because they are uncomfortable about taking ownership of a goal (what if they fail?), or because of false modesty. Listen carefully and make sure the client uses the active voice, so they take charge of their goals.

Key questions:
↓   **'How far is this goal under your control?'**
↓   **'What are you going to do?'**
↓   **'What will you be doing to achieve this goal?'**
↓   **'What can you offer others that will also make them want to help you?'**

---

6. Pay attention to the wider consequences.

Do not just focus on yourself. Every action has consequences for the wider system in which we live. Every goal we pursue will have consequences for ourselves and other people. Right from the start, we need to take this into account.

This rule applies to both destination and journey. Is the destination worthwhile? Does it lead to greater happiness? Will it lead to your life becoming more balanced? Will significant other people be hurt? Will they be benefited? What will be the cost to you and others?

There is also the journey to consider. What means will you use and what will the effects be on others? There can be a temptation for people to single-mindedly attack their goals with a ferocity that can have adverse effects on friends and family.

You can have anything you want, the saying goes, providing you are willing to pay for it. What is the cost of the goals and are you willing and able to pay it? This is not just the cost in money, but also in time and opportunity.

Key questions:

↓ **'What are the consequences for other people?' You need to take the perspective of significant others (*see page 72*) and imagine what they would think of the goals.**

↓ **'What is the cost in time, money and opportunity?'**

↓ **'What might you need to give up?'**

↓ **'How will the balance between the different aspects of your life (e.g. relationships, leisure, professional side, health) be affected when you achieve this out-**

↓ **come?'**

'What is important in your present circumstances that you might have to leave behind?'

---

7. Make an action plan.

This is what makes a dream into a goal. When you define the steps to your goal, you are putting legs on your dream.

In order to take action, you need to be motivated. This is why goals need to be challenging as well as realistic. You need to be stretched by a goal and to keep an open mind that it is possible.

A goal, especially a long-term goal, can seem daunting. The action plan divides the goal into smaller steps – each one is manageable. It is a map of the journey.

We will consider the action plan in more detail later.

The Golden Rules Applied to Outcome Goals and Process Goals

DESTINATION
(OUTCOME GOAL)

JOURNEY
(PROCESS GOAL)

POSITIVE
EVIDENCE FOR ACHIEVEMENT

PROACTIVE
FEEDBACK
How measured
How often measured
How to judge you are on track

Appropriately specified

RESOURCES
Things
People
Personal qualities
Time
Money
Role models
Books

BOTH DESTINATION AND JOURNEY:
WORTHWHILE
Measured in time
ACTION PLAN
Consequences
— for other people
— in other areas of your life
— what you have to give up
— what you want to keep

WORKING WITH GOALS

The main first step in coaching a person is to get them to define their goals. They must start from their long-term goals, and 'long term' means at least 10 years in the future.

Many people are not used to thinking so far ahead, but it is essential to do so to get a sense of direction. Only by setting long-term goals can they start to make the shorter-term goals that will support them.

Ask the client to write down at least five long-term goals (at least 10 years in the future). This is an essential part of their life planning.

It is best to make a balanced mixture of goals:

One about their career
One about their health
One about their relationships
One about money
One about personal development
Others about their spiritual development, contribution to the community, leisure or creating their ideal environment

Once they have done that then the next step is to ask them to write down some medium-term goals (five years or so into the future), then at least five two-year goals, and finally at least five one-year goals. This may take several sessions. Some clients will find it easier than others. In the Resources section there are some worksheets that you can use with clients in setting the goals (*page 173*).

Finally, to repeat the most important point of all: the goal must be worthwhile. It must align with the client's values. Goals are powered by values; it is the values that give the impetus to the journey and keep the client going when they are discouraged. The value is the real reason behind the goal. The client wants something at a deeper level.

Values

What are values? Very simple. Values are what are important to you. They are at the centre of who you are. Everyone has values. Anyone who says they do not simply does not know who they are.

Values are states of mind and principles of action and are usually abstract, for example love, honesty, fun, health, respect, freedom, loyalty, integrity, security and friendship. We value these qualities in others and we value them in ourselves.

In coaching we want to find out the values of the client, so they can fully express them in their life. You find out values by asking questions like:

↓ 'What is important to you about…?'
↓ 'What matters to you here?'
↓ 'What do you get out of doing this?'

Another good way you can find out values is to ask: 'What metaphor would you use to describe yourself when you do this? Who are you when you do this?' The metaphor that the person comes up with – for example, an Egyptologist – will have certain values implied, for example here the values of curiosity, exploration and courage.

Many people think about values in a very logical way, but values are not logical, they are an expression of who we are and people are not logical. Many people will tell you logically who they think they are, but their deeper values may be different.

Values can be context dependent, for example, what people value in relationships may not be the same as what they value in their professional life. People also tend to have core values that stay the same whatever the context.

Do not judge a client's values, even if they seem peculiar. A coach is not there to judge. A coach must respect the client's values, or not work with them.

Values are shown in behaviour, though the behaviour that shows a value will be different from person to person. Most of the time, when a person or company does something unacceptable or out of place, it is because they are unclear about the value that is generating their behaviour, and they are not sure what to do to satisfy it.

All goals are generated by values. Every single thing we want in the material world is an expression of a value that we want to satisfy. We want to travel to our destination because it is important to us. However, the journey has many pitfalls. One of the greatest is to neglect the journey too much in favour of the destination. It is crucial that you respect the value that generated the goal in the first place in the actions that you take to achieve it. You must live the value in the journey on the way to the goal.

This is the answer to the age-old question of ends and means: does the end justify the means? Some say it does and others say it does not. The answer is that ends and means are intertwined. The ends are destination goals. These are generated by one or more of our values. If we neglect the value in our haste to get to the end goal, the end goal will be hollow, if we achieve it at all. By setting the destination according to your values you automatically chart the journey that will take you there. The values that generated the goal are your compass on the journey. They make sure you achieve it in a satisfactory way.

Sometimes people set goals but try to achieve them without fulfilling the value that made the goal so attractive in the first place. For example a man may love his family and want to give them a wonderful life. He values the love of his family and works hard to earn a lot of money to bring good things to them. However, in the process, he is always out at work, so he neglects them; he becomes a stranger to his children, who become unhappy. He is also unhappy; he knows that something is wrong, but he justifies what he is doing because he is doing it 'for his family'. He is, but his actions are exactly the opposite of the reasons why he is taking them. He may achieve his goal of earning a lot of money for himself and his family, but they will all be unhappy because he didn't respect the value that generated that goal in the way that he tried to achieved it.

When we know our values, we are free to find the best way to satisfy our deepest needs. Also, living our values during the journey keeps us motivated.

The question is: how can we discover the value that is generating a particular goal?

Discovering the Value behind the Goal

Here is a coaching session to show how to find the core value behind a goal. The client's goal was to retire in 10 years' time. When we asked him what his most important value was about that, he said financial independence. This is logical and certainly it is very important, but the coach wanted to explore further the value that was generating that goal.

Coach:	Think for a moment about retirement and tell me, when you get it, what will that get for you?
Client:	I will have peace of mind.
Coach:	When you have peace of mind, what will that get for you?
Client:	I will have financial security! [The voice tone changed a little to become more animated.]
Coach:	And when you have financial security, what will that get for you?
Client:	I won't be worrying about being old. [His eyes moved down to his right and than came back again. This was negative, so it needs to be turned into a positive.]
Coach:	When you aren't worrying about being old, what will that get for you?
Client:	Happiness. [This seems like the end of the road, but the coach pressed on because she was not convinced from the client's voice tone or body language that he had reached the core value. His response still seemed a little superficial and his body was not balanced on the chair, he was leaning to one side.]
Coach:	When you have happiness, what will that get for you?
Client:	I grow! [His voice tone changed dramatically, his body posture was more balanced and he looked straight into the coach's eyes. He also used, for the first time in the session, an identity statement. He associated himself with the value 'I grow.']
Coach:	That sounds different!
Client:	But ... I thought financial security was the main reason...
Coach:	OK. So, tell me, when you have financial security, what will that get for you?
Client:	I will be able to travel and meet people in different places.
Coach:	When you travel and meet people in different places, what will that get for you?
Client:	I learn.
Coach:	When you learn, what will that get for you?
Client:	I grow!

All the roads seemed to arrive at this core value: 'I grow.'

This was the core value that was generating that goal of retirement.

The Core Value Process

Here is the process for finding the core value behind a goal:

1   What is the client's goal? What does the client want?
2   The coach takes the information and, using the client's words, asks a question that moves to a higher level (known as 'chunking up') by asking: 'When you have [the client's goal, in their own words], what does that get for you?' (Notice that the question starts with 'when' not 'if', because 'if' presupposes doubt that they will get the goal.) This question also must associate the client to the goal. In other words, they must experience in the present moment what it is like to have that goal. Another way to ask this would be: 'Imagine you have that now. What do you get from that?'
3   The client answers with another goal or value.
4   The coach now asks the same question again, using the client's answer to the previous question.
5   The client answers with another goal or value.
6   The coach and client continue this process until the client arrives at something really important. This is the value behind the goal.

It's very important to use *exactly* the client's words in this process, so for example if the client says 'peace of mind', *don't* try to paraphrase that and say for example 'tranquillity'. This may mean something very different to the client and the paraphrase will interfere with the process.

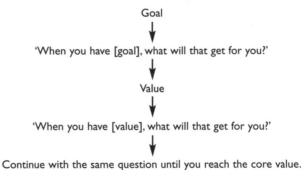

How can you know if you have found the core value?
    There are a number of ways:

↓   When the client repeats the same word a number of times during the process.
↓   When the client emphasizes some words with a gesture or a strong tonality.
↓   When the client uses an identity-level statement, with the personal pronoun 'I' plus verb. (In the example, the answer was 'I grow!')

↓ When the process goes in circles and the client is repeating the same answer that they gave before.

↓ The coach can check the core value by chunking up from the logical reason that was in place to start. (In the example, the coach utilized 'financial security' to check the value, because this was what the client thought was the main reason behind his goal.)

Once you find the value behind the goal, then achieving the goal becomes enjoyable. Without finding – and living – the value behind the goal, the journey towards it can entail years of hardship. Some people spend a miserable life looking for happiness.

This leads us to the next step. The coach needs find out the best way the client can live and respect the value in their journey towards the goal.

The session continued.

Coach: How can you make sure that you will be growing as you move towards retirement?

Client: Doing what I am doing now. Researching the best ways to improve my body, mind and soul all the way through and then checking where I am in the process and what else I can do.

Coach: How do you feel about that?

Client: I feel very good and amazed at discovering that 'growing' is the reason I am doing that. It is something I realize has strongly influenced my life and decisions.

At this stage a bystander might be thinking, 'Surely this is obvious?' The answer is that like all deep and meaningful answers to the questions of life, it's only obvious in hindsight. Also, the exact form of words carries a lot of personal meaning. If a coach had said to this client before that, 'Do you do a lot of things in your life because you value learning?', he would have probably answered, 'Yes,' but without a lot of conviction. Here he came up with the words and the words struck a deep chord with him. They came from the inside; they were not imposed on him from the outside. He connected with the value.

So, finding out the core value behind the goal and how to respect and live that during the progression towards the goal is a very simple and deep process that involves just two questions:

↓ 'When you have the goal, what will this bring for you?'

↓ How can you make sure that you will be living that value in the process?'

Notice the presuppositions behind the questions. Asking 'When you have the goal, what will this bring for you?' presupposes the goal is achieved. Asking 'How can you make sure that you will be living that value on the process?' presupposes that the client is responsible for the value and it is possible for them to live the value in the process.

THE ACTION PLAN

First of all, coaching helps the client be clear about their goals, using the seven golden rules.

Then the coach helps the client establish the core values that generated the goals and that will guide them on their journey.

Finally, they are ready to make an action plan.

Most people make an action plan by thinking forward. They start in the present and look towards the future, defining the logical steps to follow to get from here to there. We think that it is much better to plan backwards. Start from the goal. The goal is what generates the action, so the goal is the logical place to start. Many people do not start with the goal, because they are not sure they will achieve it, so they think they should start from the present. In fact, when you set a goal, the goal is what is certain. Start from the certainty of the future you desire, rather than the uncertainty of the present. When you start from the end you will get a big insight about what to do and what not to do.

Representing Time

An action plan means planning over time, so we need some way to represent time. The best way to represent time is as distance. We talk of the distant past and distant future. We see a long distance representing a long time and a short distance representing a short time. Clocks are simply a long line wound up in circles; the hands moving round that line again and again measure time. Calendars allocate a certain space for each day. So, to make an action plan, the first thing a coach needs to do is get the client to represent time as distance.

It is fundamental that the coach elicits the client's personal way to represent time. You can do that in a very straightforward way, by asking: 'Imagine a line that represents your lifetime. Point to the direction where your past seems to be. Now point to the direction where your future seems to be.' The line connecting the two points will be the 'time line'.

Future

Past

Establishing the Action Plan

Once the client has an idea of time as distance, you can work with them to establish the steps needed in their action plan. You can do the process in one of two different ways:

I The client can do the whole process by writing on a piece of paper. Get them to put the present and future on the paper – for example the present could be at the bottom and the future (with the goal) at the top, or the present in the left-hand corner and the future in the right-hand corner. Then they can write the action steps between the two. (You might need a big piece of paper!)

2 The client can mark out a time line on the floor. Ask them to point in the direction of their future (for example to their right). Establish a place for 'now' and get them to walk the time line on the floor, establishing the action steps. As they do that, you need to be writing down the action steps they say.

We will describe the process with a time line laid out on the floor with the client walking.

Action Plan Steps

↓ Establish the goal for the client and the value behind it.

↓ Let the client establish a time line.
'Where is your present?'
'Where is your future?'
'When do you want to achieve your goal?'
'How far into the future do you think it will be?'

↓ Put a piece of paper on the floor in the future with the goal written on it. This represents the moment when they will achieve their goal.

↓ Ask the client to step on that piece of paper in the 'future' and help them to really feel associated in that future moment.
'Now you are here, you have really got it!'
'See, hear and feel your achievement. What is it like? You are enjoying all the things that your outcome brings; you have everything that you planned before.'

Make sure that the client is really living that moment. Notice how their body posture and their skin colour changes. They will be really inside that future time, enjoying the feeling of achievement.

When the client is fully associated in the moment of achieving the goal, ask: 'What did you do immediately before this?' The client will tell you what had to immediately precede the goal in order for it to happen. Write this down. This needs to be an action. Some clients will describe the feelings that led them to that place. If a client gives you the feelings, then ask what action they took that gave rise to those feelings.

↓   When the client is ready, ask them to take a step back from their desired future.

↓   When they have taken a step back into that action immediately before the goal, associate them into that moment: 'What are you doing here? See hear and feel exactly what this step is like. Make it as real as possible.'

↓   Check that the client is completely associated by listening to the language that they are using. For example, they should be talking in the first person singular present tense (e.g. 'I am writing a letter' not 'Maybe I could write a letter' or 'I will be writing a letter' or 'I have been writing a letter').

↓   When you are sure that the client is associated, ask: 'What did you do immediately before this moment to make it possible?' The client will tell you. Write down that step.

↓   Ask the client to step back.

↓   Keep repeating the same process until the client arrives in the present moment. Make sure that there are at least six action steps, (this is to make sure that the action steps are sufficiently precise), each described by a verb in the present tense: 'I am doing X.'

Do not be satisfied with glib answers. With one client we took through this process, he had clearly worked out his action plan from the present to the future and was simply telling us what it was backwards. It was all happening too quickly and easily. We told him to completely forget the plan he had before and just think about what he was doing in those moments. The steps he came up with were completely different and much more useful.

↓   When the client is in the present moment, ask them what they think of the plan. Then ask them to step to the side of the time line. What do they think of it from this detached position? This gives the client two ways to evaluate. One is being in the present moment, seeing the plan ahead. The second is a more detached view, being in a way outside time and able to evaluate the steps more critically. Both views are necessary.

↓   Ask these questions from both viewpoints:
    'What do you feel about this plan?'
    'Is there anything that you would like to change in the order of the steps?'
    'Is there anything important that seems to be missing?'
    'Are there any unnecessary steps?'

↓   From the side position, ask the client to put a time for each step. 'When should each step be completed?' Write down these deadlines by each step. Check that these are realistic deadlines and not when the client 'hopes' that they will do the steps.

↓   When the client is happy about the steps and the deadlines, they should go back to the present moment and walk towards their future goal, imagining each step as they go. The coach uses their notes about the steps and deadlines to remind the client in the process. They are exploring the steps again, this way from present to future. They are also mentally rehearsing the plan and making it more real. This way of doing the action plan also breaks down the goal into manageable steps.

↓ Now the client has an action plan. Give them a task that will set them on their way and will help them accomplish the first step.

↓ Build in some celebrations! Very often we are oblivious to taking an important step because it seems like simply a step towards the next task, the way one examination qualifies you to take the next. Celebrations along the way are more motivating and keep the client in touch with their goal.

↓ Finally, how can they make sure the client is living their values in the action plan? Does the action plan represent their values? When the process is done with care and attention, the values will be in every step of the journey.

The Two Journeys

There are two parallel journeys in the action plan. One is the outward journey: a series of actions that the person will take that will change something in their environment and that other people will see. However there is also a parallel, invisible journey: the inner journey. This is a journey of feelings, of learning and of self-development. With some clients the outward journey will be the most obvious. They will easily come up with action steps and maybe not talk very much about their feelings and learning from the steps of the process. Other clients will talk about their feelings, about what they are learning and their development; their inner world is more vivid than the outward one in this process. The coach works with both at once. However, to generate an action plan, there needs to be some action, so even while exploring the inner journey, make sure there are definite steps with definite actions on the way to the goal. Learning always comes from doing something different.

We strongly suggest that you start with the client on this work with their goals and values immediately after the initial session. The initial session is when coach and client meet for the first time and negotiate how they will work together. This is our next topic.

SUMMARY

Goals
Goals are dreams with legs, they go somewhere.
Every decision that we make in life shapes our reality.
Use your fear of the unknown to direct yourself to a better future.
Setting goals is the way to take charge of your life.
We are moving from a present state to a desired state. The moment we are dissatisfied with what we have, we are on a journey towards something better.
The opposite of goal-setting is problem-thinking. This focuses on what is wrong.
A coach helps a client to explore the present and design the future.

There are two different sorts of goals.

↓   *The outcome goal: the destination, where you are heading*

↓   *The process goal: your journey, how you are going to get there*

The Seven Golden Rules of Goals

1   *Goals are expressed in the positive. This only applies to the outcome goal.*

2   *Make the goal specific.*

   Make your outcome goal as specific as possible.

   For tangible goals, describe them as exactly as possible. For abstract goals, specify the evidence that will let you know that you have the goal.

   The further into the future the goal, the less specific the client needs to be about it. Long-term goals set directions.

3   *Decide how you will get evidence and feedback for achievement.*

For an outcome goal, set the evidence that will tell you that you have achieved it. For the journey, decide on the feedback to pay attention to.

   What are you measuring?

   How will you measure your progress? Relative to yourself or relative to another person?

   How often will you measure your progress?

4   *Marshall your resources.*

   You need resources on the journey, not the destination.

   Resources can be:

   objects

   people

   time

   role models

   personal qualities

   Use resources to give leverage. Leverage is the principle of getting the most effect for the smallest effort, and it may mean stopping doing things just as much as doing them.

   Which resources do you have already?

   Which ones do you need to develop?

5   *Be proactive.*

   This principle applies to the journey, not the destination.

6   *Pay attention to ecology.*

   Ecology is the wider system in which the client lives. This rule applies to both destination and journey.

   What are the consequences for other people?

   What is the cost in time, money and opportunity?

   What is important in the present circumstances that you leave behind?

7   *Make an action plan.*
     The action plan divides the goal into smaller steps. It is the map of the journey.
     To define an action plan, you need to know the client's values.

Values
Values are what are important to you.
There are no bad values.
Values are usually stated in abstract terms.
All goals are generated by values.
One of the things that can stop you achieving your goals is not respecting your values during the process.

Find the core values that have generated a goal by asking 'What does that get for you?' until you reach the core value.
Ensure the client lives the value in achieving the goal.

The Action Plan
Start from the goal and work backwards to draw up the action plan.

ACTION STEPS

If you want to understand, act. Here are some ways to explore the ideas in this chapter. You can also use them as tasks for your client and yourself if you wish.

1   Think about a goal that you achieved in the past. Check how it fits the seven golden rules of goals.

2   Plan your life, if you have not done so already, by writing down your five most important 10-year goals. Make sure they are a balanced set, from different areas of the wheel of life (see page 59).

3   Think about a goal that you have not yet achieved.
     Find out the value behind it.
     Check whether you are respecting this value in the process of achieving this goal.
     Is the way you plan to achieve your goal congruent with the value that generated it?

4 **Define a short-term goal (one you wish to achieve in the next year), using the seven golden rules.**
   Design the action plan by working backwards from the goal.

5 **Do a stocktake of your resources.**

What skills do you have? Think of every possible context.
What knowledge do you have? Think of your education, specialist knowledge and what you have learned in the university of life.
Whom do you have a relationship with, however slight, both in the past and present? List the people you know in your work, friends past and present, family, mentors and teachers, acquaintances, etc.
When you have finished, think how any or all of these could be resources for you as a coach.

CHAPTER 4

THE FIRST SESSION

Coaching begins at the first meeting between client and coach. This is where rapport is built, trust begins and coaching starts. The initial meeting sets the scene, deals with practical details of how the coaching will work, explores the client's present situation and designs how coach and client will work together in the future.

The initial meeting is the beginning of something profound. The client has made a commitment to their own life and happiness.

The initial meeting has eight stages:

1 Building rapport and the basis of trust
2 Managing the client's expectations
3 Assessing the client and gathering information
4 Discovering the client's immediate concern
5 Designing the coaching alliance
6 Dealing with the practical arrangements
7 Committing to the coaching programme
8 Beginning coaching with the immediate issue

BUILDING RAPPORT AND THE BASIS OF TRUST

Rapport is a relationship of mutual respect and influence. There is only one chance to make a first impression, but rapport can be built all the time. Rapport comes from an honest attempt to understand the other person in their terms, to see the world from their point of view, to hear sounds in the way they hear them, to imagine what it would be like to walk in their shoes. It is not something you 'have' but a quality of the relationship. It does not mean friendship, only a willingness to be open. Rapport is not agreement – it is quite possible to have good rapport and disagree strongly. Nor is rapport an all-or-nothing quality; there are degrees. When rapport persists over time, it usually develops into trust. Rapport is natural and easy to establish on many levels. The main thing is not to do anything that will interfere with it.

Respect Values and Beliefs

In order to build rapport it is important to respect the client's beliefs and values. This does not mean that you have to agree with them, but you have to be willing to see events from their perspective and enter the coaching relationship with curiosity and a willingness to have your way of seeing things modified, otherwise you will only coach people similar to you and try to make them more like yourself.

A client is the embodiment of their values and beliefs, and you may disagree with both, but the essence of respect is accepting who the client is and how they present themselves. You may not like what they have done, but you can accept and respect what they did, given their circumstances.

If you cannot accept them at all, do not take them as a client. You have your own boundaries that need to be respected too.

Matching Behaviour

How can you show that you respect the client and want to understand them?

People like people who are like them. If you watch people who are getting on well, you will notice that they tend to match their body postures and gestures. Both will sit forward or both will sit back. Sometimes their body posture will be almost identical. Neither is deliberately copying the other, it happens naturally. This was investigated first by William Condon in the 1960s. He called it *cultural microrhythms*.

Videos of people in a good relationship show there is a dance of body language. When the videos were slowed down to separate frames of one forty-fifth of a second each, the dance of rapport was clear. One person will gesture, then a few seconds later the other person will make a similar gesture; they tend to move at the same speed and rhythm. Their body language matches.

The same is true of voice tone. People who are enjoying a good relationship tend to speak at much the same speed and with much the same volume. The speech rate (the number of speech sounds per second) equalizes. The latency period (the pause between one person stopping speaking and the other starting) tends to even out. People in very close rapport will even be breathing at the same rate.

This is rapport on the level of behaviour. It must come from a sincere desire to enter and understand the other person's model of the world. Then it is easy, powerful and natural.

So pay attention to your client on a behavioural level. If they stand, you stand. If they sit, you sit. If they move slowly, you move slowly too. Match the amount of eye contact they make. Eye contact is neither good nor bad, but people tend to give as much as they feel comfortable receiving, so match what they do. A beady stare will not create rapport, however many authorities say that eye contact is good.

Match the speed and volume of the client's voice. If they talk loudly, talk loudly as well. Pay attention to how much personal space they need; this varies from culture to culture. In Anglo-Saxon and European culture it tends to be an arm's length, hence the phrase 'to keep someone at arm's length'.

When you match body language and voice tone, the client will unconsciously understand that you are making an honest attempt to enter into their world – how they feel, how they speak, how they move and see – and so they will feel more comfortable. Matching is not mimicry; do not try to match minutiae of the client's behaviour. It will have the opposite effect to the one you intend: it makes clients uncomfortable.

Make sure you match your body and voice tone if you disagree with a client. Your words may disagree, but your gestures and voice will still tell them that you respect them and want to understand them.

In the initial meeting begin by matching:

↓   general posture
↓   speed of movement
↓   eye contact
↓   the speed of speech
↓   the loudness of speech

If the session is not going well, concentrate less on what you say and more on voice and body matching.

Matching Words

People's words reflect their thoughts and their thoughts represent their reality. So the exact words matter. Make a mental note of the important words or phrases the client uses for their values and goals (or write them down if you need to). Notice how the client will emphasize them with a gesture or a stronger voice tone. When you use the client's exact words for their important goals and values, you show them that you are paying attention to what they are thinking and what is important to them. This is known as *backtracking*.

Paraphrasing does *not* show you understand. A paraphrase gives *your* words and it comes from *your* reality. If you are lucky, it may be close enough to the client's thinking to pass muster, but why take the risk of mismatching?

When you backtrack, you restate the key points using the client's own words, and you can even match the gesture. Backtracking is useful at every stage of coaching when you want to:

↓ check for agreement
↓ build and demonstrate rapport by giving evidence that you are listening
↓ reduce misunderstanding
↓ clarify the client's values

Backtracking is simple but effective. Just as in matching body language, though, be respectful and only match what is important. If you take backtracking too far, the client will think, 'Why is the coach just repeating what I say all the time?'

Matching Thinking

What is thinking? It is different things to different people. To some people it is mostly pictures in their mind. To others it is an internal voice or a feeling that cannot be analysed too closely. In other words we see, hear and feel in our minds just as we see hear and feel with our senses in the outside world. We re-experience or *re-present* the world to ourselves using our senses:

visual	(V)	seeing
auditory	(A)	hearing
kinaesthetic	(K)	feeling
olfactory	(O)	smelling
gustatory	(G)	tasting

When we use our senses inwardly to think they are known as *representational systems* in NLP. Either we remember real past experiences or imagine possible (or impossible) future experience. You can picture yourself running for a bus (remembered visual image) or running down the canals of Mars wearing a spacesuit (constructed visual image). The first will have happened. The second will not, but you can represent both.

We do not use our representational systems in isolation, just as we do not experience the world simply through one sense. Thinking is a rich mix of all the systems, just as we experience the world through all our senses.

We use our representational systems in everything we do – remembering, planning, learning, fantasizing and problem-solving.

The visual system is how we create our internal pictures, visualize, daydream, fantasize and imagine. When you are imagining looking around one of your favourite places or remembering being on the white sandy beach on holiday, or planning how your room will look, you are using your visual system.

The auditory system is how you remember music, talk to yourself and rehear the voices of other people. Auditory thinking is often a mixture of words and other sounds. When you imagine the voice of a friend, the roar of the sea or the sound of silence, you are using your auditory system.

The olfactory system deals with creating smells and *the gustatory system* is made up of remembered and created tastes. Remember a fine meal. Think back to what it was like to smell and taste the food. You are using your olfactory and gustatory systems.

The kinaesthetic system is made up of our internal and external feelings of touch and bodily awareness. It also includes the sense of balance. The emotions are also part of the kinaesthetic system, although emotions are slightly different – they are feelings *about* something, although they are still represented kinaesthetically in the body. When you imagine balancing on a beam, the feeling of touching a smooth surface or what it is like to feel completely happy, you are using your kinaesthetic system. Sometimes the olfactory and gustatory systems are treated as part of the kinaesthetic system, as they are less important in western European and North American culture.

However, just as some of our senses are better developed and more sensitive to the outside world, so some representational systems will be better developed for thinking and we will tend to favour those systems. Most people have a preferred representation system. We think more easily and more fluently with our preferred system. This gives us an advantage in familiar situations. However, it can limit our thinking in unfamiliar situations of pressure or stress.

The preferred representational system usually links with a preferred or unusually acute sense. For example, if you pay a lot of attention to what you see, then you are likely to use the visual representational system for your thinking. People with excellent hearing may favour the auditory representational system. With a visual preference, you may be interested in drawing, interior design, fashion, the visual arts, television and film. With an auditory preference, you may be interested in language, writing, drama, music, training and lecturing. With a kinaesthetic preference you may be interested in sport, gymnastics and athletics.

So what are the practical applications for coaching? Listen to the words your client uses. Words clothe our thoughts so they can venture out of our minds and appear respectably dressed in the outside world. Words betray their mental origins. When a client says, 'I see what you mean,' they must be making a mental picture, otherwise the words do not make sense. If they say 'Let me sound out an idea with you' then they must be thinking in sounds or words. And if they say 'I can't get a grip on my life', they are thinking with the kinaesthetic representation system. Each system has its own language of sensory-based words and phrases. There is a full list of such sensory-based words and phrases in the Resources section (*see page 188*).

Following on from this, we do not think just with our brain, but with our whole body. We 'tune' our body into postures, gestures and breathing patterns to help us think in certain ways. There is a general list of how the representational systems show in our body language, postures, and breathing (*see Resources, page 184*). These are known as *accessing cues* in NLP.

In particular, the way our eyes move show clearly *how* we are thinking (but not what we are thinking). For example, when people are using their kinaesthetic system, they will tend to look down to their right. When they are talking to themselves, they will tend to look down to their left. When they visualize they will usually look up or unfocus. These are known as *eye accessing cues* (*see Resources, page 185*).

Suppose you greet a client who comes dressed in bright colours, looks up a lot when talking, has an erect posture and speaks quickly. From this you might safely assume they do a lot of visual thinking. So how do you gain the best rapport with them? Match their speed of talking – speak fast. Use lots of visual words. If they say they cannot see a way out, say that coaching will clarify their vision. Talk about expanding their horizons and giving them a fresh viewpoint. Paint a picture of a better life. When they look away or defocus, stop and let them literally see what you are saying in their mind's eye. You would also give them material to work with that represents their issues visually, like the wheel of life (*page 60*).

Perhaps your next client is a teacher. They speak continuously, fluently and easily in a pleasant voice, neither fast nor slowly. They listen to you carefully. They may rest their chin in their hands and look down to their left while asking you to tell them what you can do for them. They make it clear they enjoy music and conversation. With this client, you would speak more slowly and rhythmically and talk about discussing matters in full. You might consider scheduling more telephone coaching, or giving them audiotapes of tasks or exercises to do.

Your third client may be a little overweight. They dress in comfortable rather than fashionable clothes. They move more slowly and breathe more from their abdomen. They make themselves comfortable in the chair. They speak slowly about how they need to get a grip on their life. They may describe themselves as stuck, so you can offer them a 'helping hand'. They may pause and look down before replying. With this client, match their slow speed of talking. Talk about the importance of feelings in coaching and about how important it is to take action. Tell them how you can help them steer their life into a better channel.

These are extreme examples of three different types of person and it is seldom as clear cut as we have painted here. However, the principle is a sound one. Pay attention to a client's way of being, made up of how they think and feel and the words they use. Match these and you will get excellent rapport.

A good coach, then, needs to develop three skills:

l   The first is to listen just as much to the *kind* of words the client uses as to what they are describing. This is not as easy as it sounds — there is more to it than meets the eye, and the concept can be a slippery one, because we are used to making sense of what someone says, not how they say it.

2   The second is to make the connection between the words the client uses and the representational system they are using.

3   The third is to reply with words from the same representational system. *The exact words do matter.* When a coach replies in the same representational system, a client unconsciously perceives that they understand them at a deep level.

A Comfortable Environment

Rapport is easiest in a comfortable environment, so make your consulting room as welcoming as possible. When the environment is too hot, too cold, too noisy or too stuffy it is difficult for you and your client to concentrate. Ensure you are not disturbed by telephone calls, e-mail or visitors. Turn off the mobile telephone. The client should feel it is their space as well as yours.

Your clothes and grooming are also part of the client's surroundings, so dress comfortably and elegantly. You will be judged on the clothes you wear and how you look. This is superficial, but it happens, so it is worth taking care. If you are seeing managing directors, then dress smartly, perhaps in a suit. On the other hand, if you are offering life coaching to many different clients, then formal dress may make some feel uncomfortable.

When coaching top executives it is also important to make sure that you take them away from their 'power position' during the coaching session. When they are in their familiar office, in their familiar chair, where they are used to being in command, they feel in charge and this can make coaching more difficult.

When I (Andrea) coached the president of a big company, we first tried some sessions in his office. His secretary had strict orders that we were not to be disturbed for any reason, but it was hard for him to be open. I found it was much more productive to go somewhere else for the sessions. He relaxed more, was more open and ceased to be so driven by work. He enjoyed the sessions more and they were more productive.

Gaining Trust

Rapport can be built quickly and lost quickly, but trust takes time. To gain a person's trust, you need to demonstrate some essential qualities from the first session onwards.

↓   Be real. Don't pretend to be someone you are not or to feel something you do not feel. You are not perfect; you are human, like your client.

↓   Be sincere. Keep your word. If you say you will do something, then do it. If you do not, have a very good reason why not.

↓   Be competent. Be able to carry out your promises.

↓   Be honest. Tell the truth as you see it – do not waste the client's time or your own. However, always tell the truth in a way that is respectful. Admit when you do not understand and when you do not know the answer to something. Risk appearing human – this will make you more trustworthy.

↓ Be congruent. Congruence is when your words and actions match. If you are congruent, you will not give mixed messages to the client. The more you are in conflict with yourself, the less available you are for the client. You will find it hard to give a client your full attention and ask clear questions if they are describing a conflict that you feel in yourself. Sometimes a client's issue may raise some uncomfortable emotions in you. Sometimes you need to say that you will not discuss their issue because it is also an issue for you. You need to wait until you are over it. Having a coach of your own is a tremendous help in this situation.

↓ Be there! Turn up on time. Be present in mind and body; give the client your full attention.

MANAGING THE CLIENT'S EXPECTATIONS

You need to prepare the client for coaching. What do they expect?

Some clients expect therapy, with the coach delving into their past. Other clients expect the coach to tell them what to do. You should explain that you will do your best to work with them so that they have a fuller happier life, fulfil their goals and live their values, but they own the process and the results. Explain what happens in the coaching process and give them a written summary that they can refer to.

You can also warn clients that sometimes you will interrupt them during the coaching session. Coaching is not the place for a client to tell rambling stories that shore up their present unsatisfactory situation. Tell them that sometimes you will interrupt them because you believe the conversation is not in their best interests. Ask them to let you know if they are offended at the time. This should be sufficient to get permission for any intrusion you feel is necessary.

Confidentiality

Make it clear to the client that you will not discuss anything they tell you with a third party without their permission. When the client is paying for the coaching directly, this is no problem. When the client's employer is paying for the coaching, then the issue is more complicated, as the company will expect some feedback. Be careful in this case. Set out an agreement with the company *before* you start the coaching. There are several possibilities.

First, you could agree on the outcomes of the coaching and as long as the results are good, the company need not know the details of the coaching. For example, you are employed to coach a manager who is underperforming. You agree in advance on how much the manager needs to improve. When this is achieved, the job is done and the company needs no details of the client's problems or the coaching you did. Providing you have some way of assessing the results in terms of improved effectiveness, you can still keep the client discussions entirely confidential.

I (Joseph) have been in this situation. I was engaged to coach a senior member of an executive team. He was in conflict with the other board members. They all saw him as a problem. I made it clear to the company that I would not disclose any of the coaching discussions without my client's permission, and they agreed.

When we started the initial session, the client was well aware of what was happening and he did not agree that he was causing all the difficulties! It became more and more clear that his position in the company was difficult, mostly because of the way the company was structured. His department's interests were often in conflict with other departments, and he was very assertive when he argued for them. He was a very intelligent man, extremely competitive and energetic, and it was true that he also had personal clashes with some of the other directors. Yet one coaching session of four hours was all we needed to resolve the problem. He realized how the structure of the company was putting him in a difficult position and knew what steps to take to change it. He became more aware of exactly how the personality clashes were happening, how they were triggered and what he could do to avoid them.

A second possibility is to agree to give the company feedback, but to let the client see it first and agree that it can be passed on. You then need to discuss with the client what feedback to give the company. Say the client talks about a problem at home or work that is affecting their job performance. You would not share this confidence without permission, even if it is extremely important and affecting the client's work.

If you, the company and the client cannot agree in advance on what feedback to give or how to give it, then do not take on the coaching. The client is unlikely to be completely open with you if they think that what they say will be reported to their managers. You will get a sanitized version of the problem and will not be able to do very much.

This touches on ethical standards. Ethics is about your *internal* standards. Your standards affect your actions and your actions are what make you the person you are. We are all participants in the human drama, not scientific observers looking on from the sidelines. What we do affects others and ourselves. If you were to break a confidence, even if it were never discovered, it would still have an effect on you – you would know.

We also have external standards that we expect from others and what others expect from us. These standards are our ethics from the outside. Your standards will apply to how you coach, your training, ability, peer supervision and qualifications. Coaching is a fairly new profession, so standards are very important; they are the public face of coaching. Clients expect qualified, competent coaches. If you are a member of a coaching organization or have had certification training such as ours then you will want to work to ethical standards. Public high standards are a guarantee to the customer of the quality of your work. Such standards enhance your credibility. If you are a member of a professional body with clear standards, this will help you to get clients. (Our certification standards and ethics and core coaching competencies are published; *see Resources, pages 161–8*.)

You will also make an agreement with the client regarding fees, times and methods of coaching. This is a separate issue from standards and is different from coach to coach. We give some guidelines on this in the Resources (*page 176*).

ASSESSING THE CLIENT AND GATHERING INFORMATION

Initial Information

At your first meeting, if not before, you need to obtain the client's basic contact information:

    name
    address
    telephone number
    mobile number
    fax number
    e-mail address
    website

If the client is employed, then you will also need:

    employer's name and address
    telephone number
    fax number
    website

Have a printed form ready to take down all this information.

Curriculum Vitae

Many career coaches work with outplacement agencies to find clients work and coach them in career planning and getting the skills for their new appointment. In this case you will need a more detailed CV, for example:

academic record and professional qualifications

employment history

companies the client has worked for

title and job description of the positions they held

turnover and profit of that company (where appropriate)

the range of services and products the client was responsible for

the customer profile for that company

experience (if any) of floating companies on the stock market

any non-executive directorships

It is best to design a form to get the information you need.

All this information tells you little about the client, however, except what they have done and how to contact them. Now you need to know more about the client as a person.

The Client

Here are some essential topics to discuss with the client. Which areas you concentrate on will depend on the type of coaching you do and the immediate issue for the client. All may be important.

The following are questions you probably will not ask directly, but they point to areas that you may want to know about in order to coach effectively. When appropriate, you can explore these issues over the course of the coaching relationship.

Career

A career is work over time. Not all clients think like this. Some may take different types of work without a common thread.

What does the client do?

What do they think about their work?

What interest are they pursuing in their work?

What have they done to protect their career?

What are they doing to develop their career?

Do they feel stuck?

Do they have regrets?

Is their work providing for their income needs?

Relationships

The quality of a person's relationships reflects the quality of their life and happiness.

> What sort of relationships does the client have?
> Are they married?
> Do they have a family?
> Do they have many close friends?
> To whom are they closest?
> Are they happy with their relationships?

Health and energy

How the client feels physically and their general level of energy are important. A coach is not a doctor, so you are not diagnosing, but if you feel a client needs a physical check-up and medical treatment in addition to coaching, then encourage them to visit their doctor.

> How is their health?
> What do they do to maintain their health?
> Are they worried about their health?
> Do they feel well?
> How is their energy level?

Financial situation

> How do they think about money?
> Are they happy with the money they earn?
> Do they have sufficient savings to tide them through an unexpected crisis?
> How do they look after their financial security?

Goals and values

> What do they want in life?
> What is important to them?
> What are they doing to achieve their goals?
> Why do they do what they do?

Commitment to self-development, balance of life and spiritual development

What sort of spiritual life do they have?
What do they invest in their self-development?
How do they contribute to the wider community?

Leisure activities and interests

What hobbies do they have?
What do they enjoy doing to relax?
What do they read?
Are their hobbies solitary or shared?

The immediate concern

Why have they come to coaching?
What do they want from coaching?
What do they think that coaching can bring to them?

The Wheel of Life

An excellent coaching tool for assessing the client's present position and balance of life is the wheel of life (*see Resources, page 159*). The wheel is divided into eight quadrants:

physical environment (surroundings and possessions)
health
career
relationships
romance
self-development
finances
fun and recreation

The client fills in the wheel with a percentage that measures their *satisfaction* with each issue *at the present moment*. Not absolute value, only satisfaction.

For example, a client earning £20,000 a year might be 90 per cent satisfied with their finances, but a millionaire might only be 50 per cent satisfied.

Here is the wheel of a client:

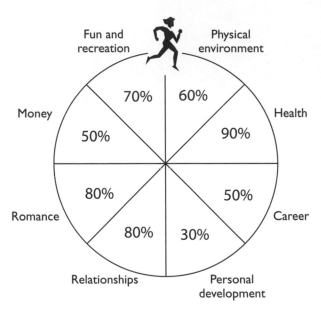

The Wheel of Life

The wheel of life
===

The wheel of life

This wheel shows:

> 60 per cent satisfaction with the client's physical environment
> 90 per cent satisfaction with their health
> 50 per cent satisfaction with their career
> 30 per cent satisfaction with their self-development
> 80 per cent satisfaction with their relationships
> 80 per cent satisfaction with their romance
> 50 per cent satisfaction with their finances
> 70 per cent satisfaction with their fun and recreation

Imagine this wheel on a car taking the client through their life's journey. It would give a bumpy ride. Their life is not balanced. Obvious areas for work are self-development, career and finances, even if these did not figure in their immediate concern.

It is also interesting to check how an improvement in one area can improve other areas as a 'side-effect'. For example, if this client pays more attention to their self-development this can have a very good effect on their career and so improve their income. Often there is a leverage point in the wheel of life – the point where a little effort in one area can have the greatest results in that area and in other areas. In this case, self-development is the leverage point for improving the other two areas, which would need no direct effort at all.

Doing a wheel of life with your clients every month gives good feedback on the coaching. Satisfaction will usually increase gradually (sometimes dramatically).

The goal is not to be 100 per cent satisfied with every aspect of life. Whatever our level of satisfaction, we become accustomed to it sooner or later and want more. Sometimes a client becomes more dissatisfied as the coaching progresses. For example, initially a client may be 80 per cent satisfied with their financial situation, but after a little coaching they realize that they should set their sights much higher. They feel they deserve more and are being underpaid for their work. Their financial satisfaction could then drop to 50 per cent.

Informal Assessment

How you assess a client will be personal to you. Do not judge, approve or condemn, just observe and listen to the client. Let them be themselves. What sort of person are they?

How do they see, hear and feel the world?

How do they interpret their experiences?

What is their prevailing emotional mood?

What sort of stance do they take towards others?

How do they view their rights and responsibilities and which do they see as the more significant?

What does the client look like?

How do they dress?

What gestures do they use habitually?

What is their voice like?

Is it loud or soft?

Do they speak fast or slowly?

What typical speech patterns do they have?

What habitual words or phrases do they use?

What eye movements do they use?

How much eye contact do they give?

Noticing these details will help you get rapport by matching body language and voice tone. As you listen to your client you will also start to get a sense of who they are and how they think.

Are they impulsive or cautious? Are they likely to hold back and think before taking action?

Do they talk in general terms or do they pay attention to detail?

Are they interested in ideas or are they more pragmatic?

How dependent are they on the opinions of others?

How much attention do they pay to feedback?

One friend of ours told us how he deals with feedback about being late. 'I listen to what other people say. Then I think of the advantages of doing what I do anyway. Then I decide whether I will change.' He is a man who will always decide for himself. Other people are much more dependent on outside feedback and will often assume they are wrong and others are right regardless.

Some clients notice what is wrong. They will tell you exactly what is wrong with their life and exactly why helpful suggestions will not work. Such clients may be 'yes butters'. You make a suggestion and their first reaction is 'Yes, but...' In the initial session, you need do nothing except listen and observe. Later, you will need to deal with this (*see page 89*). Once you know how your client thinks you will be able to help them.

When clients first come to you, they are often dissatisfied and frustrated. They will describe their situation in different sorts of metaphors. Some clients will say they are stuck. Others may say they are blocked, or caught in a quicksand, they feel trapped and they can't break free. These are all kinaesthetic metaphors. Other clients may say that they are looking for a way out, but cannot find it, or they cannot see any solution, or their horizons are too narrow. These are visual metaphors. Auditory metaphors are more rare, but we have heard some people say that they feel as though everyone is shouting at them all at once.

The first thing for a coach to do is to match the client's language. If they say they feel stuck, then talk in general terms about how you can get them moving again. If they say they cannot see a way out, say you can show them one. If they say their life is too full of meaningless chatter, then offer to quiet the din so they can think clearly. This way the client will unconsciously perceive you understand their situation. You are speaking their language.

Once you are in rapport with the client, lead them to another representational system. Ask the client who feels stuck what it would be like to see their situation from another point of view. Ask the client who cannot see a way out to imagine taking steps forward. These simple interventions will help the client to think about their situation in a new way.

DISCOVERING THE CLIENT'S IMMEDIATE CONCERN

The client's immediate concern will be obvious early in the session. Some clients feel they are not achieving all they could. They want to move forward, but are not sure how. They will say what they want from coaching and will respond immediately to work on goals.

Other clients are more aware of the difficulties in their life. They sense a problem and that is why they come to coaching. These clients still need to work on goals, but they need a direction and a destination to move towards before they can move away from their uncomfortable present.

Some immediate concerns are about learning new skills. This may only take one or two sessions. As a coach, you will clarify the outcome, get the values behind it, explore any beliefs that might be hindering it and then design an action plan to build or increase the skill. Afterwards, you may need to be available on the other end of a telephone for a few weeks to provide support.

A second type of client will need a more complex conversation over several sessions. They may have limiting beliefs and difficult circumstances that you need to work on together. Their goals will need clarification and the coaching may involve many aspects of their life and may take weeks or months.

Finally, there are those clients who need a more profound conversation and want a fundamental change. They are more likely to want life coaching. The kinds of issues that might precipitate this sort of coaching would be a career change or raising children. This coaching could take several months.

Whatever the issue, you need to explore the following questions with the client:

How will you both know that the coaching programme is successful? You both need to be clear about what constitutes success for the coaching.

What will the client need to do?

What will they need to stop doing? What habits do they have that are maintaining the obstructions and what is present in their life that is hindering them? The client will need to evaluate their habits, stop some and build others.

What will the client need to do more of?

What will the client need to do differently?

What exercises and tasks can you assign that will allow them to do this? Even at the initial session, you may get an idea about what these tasks might involve.

DESIGNING THE COACHING ALLIANCE

Now that you have told the client what coaching is and what it isn't, you are in a good position to design the 'coaching alliance'. How does the client like to be coached? How can the two of you work together to obtain the best results?

One way you can design this alliance is to give the client a piece of paper at the first session with two headings:

Coaching works well for me when the coach does these things…
Coaching does not work well for me when the coach does these things…

Then you have a good idea of what suits the client. This helps you both to design the alliance.

The coach needs to be more flexible than the client. When a coach cannot change their style to suit different clients, they will always be limited to a certain type of client.

The alliance makes it possible for the client to be accountable for the results of the coaching. They own their solutions; they are responsible for them. If the coach tells the client what to do, the client will not own the solution. This does not mean that a coach cannot make suggestions, sometimes strongly, and help the client come to their own solution through questions, suggestions and tasks. However, the client can always choose.

This is very important. Unless the client realizes they own the results and are accountable for the coaching, they will expect the coach to change them. If there is a lack of progress, they are likely to blame the coach for it and the coach may fall into the trap of feeling responsible for it.

Coaching is an alliance. This is most clear in sports coaching. The sports coach works with the athlete, but it is the athlete who stands on the winner's podium, not the coach. The athlete gets the glory and the medals. The coach has been essential, but they take no public credit.

DEALING WITH THE PRACTICAL ARRANGEMENTS

There are practical arrangements to be dealt with – how and when you coach and how much you charge. There are many possibilities to decide upon: the cost, face-to-face and/or telephone coaching, the times and duration of the coaching. These issues are discussed in the Resources (*page 179*).

COMMITTING TO THE COACHING PROGRAMME

Coaching works if both coach and client commit to it. Do not accept a client unless you are prepared to help them wholeheartedly and respect them for who they are. If you are uncertain, or you feel that they have psychological issues that would be more suited to therapy or counselling, then refer them to a good therapist or counsellor. You can be honest and say that you do not feel that you are the right person to help them at this time and that you think they would be better off seeing someone else.

The client also needs to commit to the coaching. This is not simple. The client is already committed to many things in their life, for example work, friends, family and hobbies. You are asking them to commit to one more. Where will coaching fit into their existing commitments?

To give a congruent commitment, you both need to explore the possible obstructions and hindrances to the coaching programme. Looking at possible obstacles is not being negative or pessimistic. When you both know what could stop the programme then you are better prepared to commit to it.

↓ What could interrupt this coaching programme for you?

↓ How does coaching fit into what you are already doing?

↓ What will you do if the coaching seems to be going too slowly, or gets boring or pointless?

Commitment is not just intellectual; it is also emotional. The client will only take action and continue in the coaching relationship if they are emotionally engaged. Intellectual commitment alone is not enough.

When you start the programme, explore the client's realistic commitment to it:

↓ First say what could happen in the coaching programme if it is successful. This offers motivation and gives you both a goal for the programme.

↓ Then declare your own commitment to the programme.

↓ Ask for your client's commitment. This means they will be on time for their calls or their sessions and will perform the tasks that you agree on between you.

BEGINNING COACHING WITH THE IMMEDIATE ISSUE

Now you've made the commitment, let's get to work! Starting work on the immediate issue in the first session will give the client a sense of movement and motivation. Whatever the issue, begin working with goals. The wheel of life is also a good first exercise.

Give the client homework at the end of the session so you will have something to discuss at the beginning of the next session.

SUMMARY

The initial coaching meeting has eight stages:

1 **Building rapport and the basis of trust**
   Respect the client's beliefs and values.
   Match body language and voice tone in an honest way with the intention of understanding the client.
   Backtrack important words and values to check for agreement, demonstrate rapport, clarify values and reduce misunderstanding.
   Match the client's thinking style by looking for representational system accessing cues. Listen for sensory-based words and match them.
   Provide a comfortable and welcoming environment.
   Build trust over time. Be real, competent and honest.

2 **Managing the client's expectations**
   Let the client know what to expect.
   Tell them about coaching.
   Respect their confidences.
   Be clear before you start about the feedback arrangements if the client is not your employer.
   Adhere to professional coaching standards and ethics.

3 **Assessing the client and gathering information**
   Take basic contact information.
   Make an informal assessment of the client's personality. What sort of person are they? What do they want?

Take information about:
>   *their career*
>   *their relationships*
>   *their health and energy*
>   *their financial situation*
>   *their goals and values*
>   *their commitment to self-development, balance of life and spiritual development*
>   *their leisure activities and interests*
>   *their immediate concern*

Take a detailed CV if necessary.
Use the wheel of life to explore their current balance of life and levels of satisfaction.

4 Discovering the client's immediate concern
What brings the client to coaching?
How will they know that the coaching programme is successful?
What will they have to do differently?
What will they have to stop doing? What habits are maintaining the obstructions in their life and what in their life is maintaining those habits?

5 Designing the coaching alliance
How does the client like to be coached?
Make an agreement. The client owns the results of the coaching.

6 Dealing with the practical arrangements
Discuss payments, timing and scheduling appointments.

7 Committing to the coaching programme
Explore the client's realistic commitment to the programme.
Talk about what could happen when the programme is successful.
Confront and clarify any potential hindrances:
>   *What could interrupt this coaching programme for the client?*
>   *How does coaching fit into what you are already doing?*
>   *What will the client do if the coaching seems to be going too slowly or gets boring or pointless?*

Declare your own commitment to the programme.
Ask for your client's commitment.

8 Beginning coaching with the immediate issue
Leave the client with questions and homework and schedule the next appointment.

ACTION STEPS

If you want to understand, act. Here are some ways to explore the ideas in this chapter. You can also use them as tasks for your client and yourself if you wish.

1   Watch people talking in restaurants (not in an obvious way!)
    Can you tell who is in rapport?
    Why do you think so?

2   With whom would you like to get on with better in your life?
    Next time you meet them, be very curious about why you do not get on with them as well as you want. Listen to their verbal language and observe their body language. Do some body language and voice matching. Does this make a difference?

3   When next you are on the telephone, start by matching the voice level and speed of the caller. When you want the conversation to end, mismatch, ie speak more loudly or softly, or faster or slower. Does it make the conversation easier when you match and make it easier to stop when you mismatch?

4   The next time you have a professional conversation, listen carefully and then backtrack the four main important points that they made when they spoke. Use their exact words to backtrack the key points. Notice if this makes the conversation any easier.

5   Find out your preferred representational system if you do not know it already. You can do this by recording yourself talking about something that engages you for a few minutes. Then listen to the recording and notice which sensory-based words you tend to use the most. You can also think about your general posture, gestures, breathing pattern and general interests.

6   When you know your own preferred representational system, discover the preferred system of each of your clients. Do you find you get on better with those who share your preferred system?

7   Complete a wheel of life for yourself today. What does it tell you about the balance of your life? What is the most important thing to start working with today?

8   **How would you like to be coached? Make a list of the things that would make coaching go well for you if you were a client. What does this tell you about your own coaching style with your clients?**

⇨ ⇨

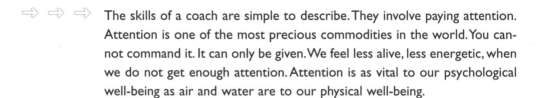

CHAPTER 5

THE ART OF COACHING

⇨ ⇨ ⇨ The skills of a coach are simple to describe. They involve paying attention. Attention is one of the most precious commodities in the world. You cannot command it. It can only be given. We feel less alive, less energetic, when we do not get enough attention. Attention is as vital to our psychological well-being as air and water are to our physical well-being.

From the very first coaching session, paying attention to the client involves two skills:

↓ calibration
↓ listening

CALIBRATION

Calibration is an NLP term which means accurately recognizing how another person is feeling by reading non-verbal signals.

Calibration is the difference between seeing, noticing and observing. Most people just *see* another person. Seeing is only letting the electromagnetic wavelength of light register on the eye. So a person may see someone else's eye movements, their gestures and their clothing, but will not draw any meaning from them.

The next level is noticing. If you notice something, what you see becomes significant. There was an eye movement. What did it mean? There was a sharp hand gesture. What does that mean? It has meaning for the client, therefore it must have meaning for the coach too.

The last level is observing. At this level, you can calibrate. Now not only do you notice but you also see patterns. For example, you observe that when the client is upset they tense their mouth and forehead in a subtle way. The left side of their mouth turns up. Their voice tone becomes a little harder and they speak more quickly. You see this consistently. You also notice that when they talk about their boss, you observe the same patterns. Are they angry with their boss? Probably. You are in a position to ask, and your client may be amazed at your intuition, but it is careful observation and calibration that allowed you to go so quickly to the issue.

Your clients will tell you about their lives in every shrug of their shoulders, every sigh, every glance to the side – if you are looking. Their voices will show their hopes and dreams, what is important to them, when they are angry, when they are sad, when they are happy or bored. Their body language is rich with meaning and messages. Watch their eye movements. Watch their gestures. When they talk about time, do they gesture to their right or left? Do they gesture to behind or in front? Once you calibrate a client, you know them very well. You understand them, and this will help them to understand themselves.

LISTENING

Listening seems simple. However, when you pay close attention to your client and listen carefully without judgement, interpretation or distortion, it is a profound experience. There are four levels of listening:

1   Hearing
    The most superficial level is hearing. Hearing registers the sound waves of another person's voice. You can hear someone talk and be thinking of something else or even doing something else. You do not have to pay attention to them to hear them. A coach should never be at this stage.

2   Listening to
    The second level is listening to the client, but with a question in mind: 'What does this mean to me?' You are listening from inside your own experience, using someone else's experience to trigger your own memories. They might be telling you of a conversation with their partner and you might be thinking back to a similar conversation you had with your partner. This is the everyday level of listening and it is adequate for everyday conversations, but not for coaching.

3   Listening for
    The third level is listening for something in what the client says. The coach may have an idea and is filtering what the client says and selecting in order to make a judgement. The coach may be engaging in internal dialogue with themselves in order to do this.

4 Conscious listening

Conscious listening is deep listening with the minimum of judgement. You keep yourself out of the way. There is the minimum of internal dialogue. This is the level where your intuition can work best.

There are three enemies of conscious listening:

↓ *Internal dialogue.* When you are listening to yourself, you cannot listen to your client. Your internal dialogue may not even be about what the client is saying but about something else entirely: 'Have I left the kettle on?' 'What's for lunch?' 'I'm thirsty.' 'I wonder what film is on TV tonight.' This sort of internal dialogue guarantees that you are hearing the client but not listening. Even if your internal dialogue *is* about what the client is saying, that only takes you to level three. So let the client talk to you, don't talk to yourself.

↓ *Muscle tension.* It is difficult to listen when you are tense. So if you find your attention wandering, relax. Also, make sure you are comfortable – physical discomfort will distract you as well.

↓ *A focused stare.* Your mind will be more open and more receptive if you use your whole visual field, so soften the focus of your eyes and widen your vision. Take in as much as you can with a soft, open focus.

PERCEPTUAL POSITIONS

A coach is the master of different perspectives. A good coach knows their own goals and boundaries but also has the ability to see the world from the viewpoint of the client and to take an objective view. In NLP these three perspectives are known as *perceptual positions.*

↓ *First position* is your own reality, your own view of any situation, your beliefs, feelings, opinions, interests, preoccupations and values. Mastery in coaching comes from a strong first position, that is knowing yourself, your goals, values and boundaries.

↓ *Second position* means taking client's point of view. It means developing the ability to make a creative leap of your imagination to understand the world from another person's perspective, to think in the way they think. When you adopt second position you need to understand the client's point of view, although this doesn't mean that you need to agree with them. Second position is the basis of coaching because it leads to empathy and rapport.

↓ *Third position* is taking a detached perspective outside your view and the client's view. There you can see the connection and relationship between the two viewpoints.

We would like to add one further perspective to these three.

↓   *Fourth position* is the perspective from the system in which the client is acting. It could be the business in which the client works. When you are doing business coaching you need to know how the client's actions impact the larger system of the business, and how in turn the business system constrains what the client can do and influences their thinking.

Another possible fourth position would be the client's family. How do the client's actions impact them? How does the family limit or empower the client's goals?

Fourth position is also about ecology, about checking the impact that the client's decisions will have on other people who will be influenced by the change.

Often coaching will involve teaching the client to take different positions in order to deal with a problem. For example, the ability to take second position is fundamental to good relationships, so you may need to coach a client to be better at second position if they have trouble in their relationships. On the other hand, if a client is always being pushed around and feels that other people's goals are more important than their own, you may need to strengthen their first position. And in third position, it's possible for them to have a more objective view of the situation and to find the leverage point that can lead to the results they want.

All positions are useful. They are invaluable resources. Many people are very adroit at one position, but not so good at taking another. The best understanding comes from taking all of them. A coach needs to be adept in all positions. We will be discussing how to use these positions later.

SUMMARY

Pay attention to the client.
Calibrate the client – accurately recognize their state by reading their non-verbal signals. There are three levels of calibration: seeing, noticing and observing.
Listen carefully to the client. There are four levels of listening: hearing, listening to, listening for and conscious listening.
There are three enemies of good listening:
> *unnecessary muscle tension*
> *internal dialogue*
> *a focused stare*

A coach must be able to take different perspectives and teach the client to take them if necessary.

1   *First position is the person's own reality – their goals, values and interests.*
2   *Second position is being able to appreciate another person's reality from their point of view.*
3   *Third position is seeing the relationship more objectively in a detached and resourceful way.*
4   *Fourth position is the point of view from the system the client is in, e.g. their business or family. It is a good position from which to check the impact of their goals on the system.*

ACTION STEPS

If you want to understand, act. Here are some ways to explore the ideas in this chapter. You can also use them as tasks for your client and yourself if you wish.

1   Pick a conversation that is not important and listen to that person with a completely open mind, with no internal dialogue. Do not try to understand or interpret. What new insights did you get about that person?

2   Which of the three perceptual positions do you suspect it is easiest for you to adopt?

3   If you prefer one position, make a list of the benefits of having that position strongly. Then make a list of the drawbacks. (For example, if you have a strong first position, you know your own mind, but might be considered opinionated. A strong second position gives you great empathy, but can lead you to neglect your own interests. A strong third position gives you objectivity at the risk of appearing 'distant'.) Then make a list of the benefits that you would get from developing the other two positions.

CHAPTER 6

QUESTIONS ARE THE ANSWER

The initial session is over and you have a new client. What now? Coaching has a structure. Here is the overall picture:

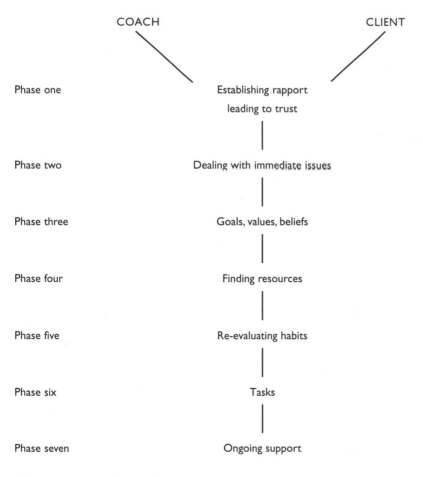

The structure of coaching

Establishing rapport comes first. Begin this at the initial session and pay attention to it during every phase of the coaching programme. Over time rapport develops into trust.

The second step in our overall structure is dealing with the client's immediate issue. This is the main reason why they come to coaching. Sometimes the coaching keeps with that issue throughout. The client wants a problem resolved, for example, or wants to improve a skill and the coaching focuses on that. More often, though, it broadens out into other issues, touching many aspects of the client's life.

Once you have started to explore the client's immediate problem you enter phase three: establishing the client's goals and values. This is a rich phase. Goals and values are the colours with which the client paints the picture of their life. They are the musical notes in their life song. Many clients' lives are more drab and silent than they need to be. The coach opens the doors to a richer, more colourful world.

In this phase coach and client work together, turning the client's dreams into reality, starting with long-term goals. They turn problems into goals and establish an action plan to achieve them. They also work together to find the energy behind the goals, the engine that drives the client forward – their values. All coaching is based on client's goals and values. Their life moves towards their goals, powered by their values.

How does a coach work this transformation? Mostly by asking good questions.

THE ART OF QUESTIONS

Questions do many things. In the initial session the coach asks questions to get information and establish facts. In the following phases, the coach asks questions to explore the client's beliefs and values, to drill down to find out how the client is thinking, what they want, why they want it and what might be limiting them from getting it.

Questions have a strange quality – you cannot not respond to a question. They force you to think about your experience. Even if you answer 'I don't know', you have still had to think about the question and examine your experience in order to come up with that answer.

Questions are like spotlights that shine into dark places. A good question will illuminate new areas. When you ask a client a powerful question, you give them the opportunity to sift through their experience and resources in a different way and find answers that they did not think they had. Clients have usually been looking for answers in places they are familiar with, but the answers do not lie there, otherwise the client would have found them already.

There is a Zen story about a man who is looking frantically under a streetlight. A passer-by stops to help him.

'What are you looking for?' he asks.

'My keys,' replies the man.

'Where did you lose them?' asks the Good Samaritan.

'Oh, I lost them in the house,' replies the man.

'Just a minute,' says the helpful stranger, 'if you lost them in the house, why are you looking for them out here in the street?'

'Because it is dark in the house,' replies the man. 'I can't see. Out here it is light, so I am looking here.'

Coaches ask questions that shine light in the right places.

One of the most interesting questions I (Andrea) have ever been asked was during an interview to discover how I do coaching and training. Some people were modelling my coaching and training ability. They were interested not just in seeing me training and coaching but also knowing my mental strategies and goals and values about coaching and training. I had been answering their questions without thinking too much, because I had thought about these things before. However, the last question of the interview made a difference: 'What metaphor would you use to describe yourself as a coach and trainer?'

This really made me think … I let my mind wander free, just waiting for something to come. Suddenly I saw myself as an explorer of ancient pyramids, and that made a lot of sense to me.

'Why a pyramid explorer?' they asked.

'Because when you know where to look, you can find treasures inside places where nobody has been before. I see people like temples, with hidden treasures just waiting to be brought out!'

This was my metaphor for coaching: a pyramid explorer, someone who brings out the best. I realized that because of a good question at the right moment.

Presuppositions

The metaphor of the question as a powerful searchlight is an apt one. Questions do shine light, but equally they leave other areas in darkness. In other words, questions direct the client's attention towards certain issues and therefore away from other issues. How do they do this? Mainly through the presuppositions implicit in the questions. A presupposition is an assumption that has to be accepted as true before you can think about the question.

All questions contain presuppositions. You either have to accept these presuppositions if you are to answer the question, or you have to ask a question about the question. For example, when a coach asks a client 'What do you want?', this presupposes that the client wants something. The client may give their goals or say they do not know; both answers mean the client has accepted the presupposition. Alternatively, the client could reply, 'I don't want anything.' This answers the question in a different way – by rejecting the presupposition behind the question. They might question the presupposition itself by asking, 'What makes you think I want anything?'

One part of the art of asking powerful questions is to build the most empowering presuppositions into them. Many people ask questions with presuppositions that have no use or are harmful.

For example, consider the question 'Who's to blame for this?' This question has two assumptions. First, that blame exists and second that the fault can be allocated. These are not empowering presuppositions. Blame looks backwards. It finds fault in people in order to explain how the problem was created. Even if blame can be allocated, this does nothing to solve the problem. Furthermore, when a client believes in blame, they have to assume that whenever something goes wrong, someone is at fault and perhaps should be punished. They have to believe that problems do not happen, people cause them. In this view, if blame cannot be pinned on *someone* else, then the client themselves must be to blame, and this is not a liberating assumption either, though a positive by-product of this is the illusion of control – there is an explanation for everything.

The concept of blame has no part in coaching.

Here is another example of a disempowering question: 'Why is he trying to hurt you? This looks like a simple request for information, but it has an assumption that a man is trying to hurt you – and he means to hurt you. A coach cannot assume this unless the client has said so.

A final example: 'How long have you allowed this situation to continue?' The assumption here is that the situation is under your control. If the situation is a bad one then this adds insult to injury, for you have been making efforts to resolve it, but have not succeeded. In coaching this question can also be interpreted as a rebuke that a client knew the situation was bad and deliberately allowed it to continue.

All these examples have been of disempowering assumptions. Examples of empowering questions would be (assumptions in brackets):

↓   'Of all the resources you have, which do you think would be most effective in helping this situation?' (You have many resources and can choose. Also, your resources can help the situation.)

↓   'What stops you making the change?' (You can make the change.)

↓   'How many things can you learn from this?' (You can learn from this.)

Always ensure your questions contain useful and empowering assumptions.

Timing

Timing is crucial in asking questions, just like in telling a joke. A question might evoke a blank stare one moment, but a 'Eureka' insight if asked five minutes later. How do you know when to ask a question?

Timing your questions well is partly down to intuition. Intuition is knowing when to do something without consciously knowing how you know. You can train your intuition in two ways.

1   *Listen!* Relax. Turn off your internal dialogue. Ask yourself, 'What does this client need right now?' You may have a great question in mind, but is it right for the client now?

2   *Calibrate the client.* If you pay attention to their body language and voice tone, you will know when they are open to a question. A good coach can change the second half of a question based on the client's non-verbal response to the first half.

As you become better at listening and calibration, you will start to time your questions well because you have got into the habit of listening beyond the words and noticing the non-verbal signals. When you do these things naturally, you will not be aware of doing them, but you will act on what you see and hear. What you will notice consciously is how much better your questions are.

Honesty

How will you know a client is giving an honest answer? How will you know if they are only telling you what they think you want to hear?

First, you will have explained how coaching works in the initial meeting. You will have told the client that by not answering a question honestly they will be the loser, because the coaching is for their benefit. However, they are always entitled to refuse to answer.

Secondly, you will be calibrating your client, so you will be able to see from their body language and voice tone when they are uneasy or unsure about an answer. Then you may choose either to leave that area of enquiry or to probe further.

Thirdly, a coach's questions come from an open and honest attitude of curiosity. A coach models honesty for the client. When the client sees this, they will give honest responses.

Lastly, you can ask some powerful follow-up questions like:

'What else did you observe?'
'How would you say that if you did not care what I thought about it?'
'Is there anything more you want to explore beyond what you have already said?'

Building Rapport with Questions

Questions can be used to build rapport. Even a challenging question can be asked with respect and need not break rapport.

There are two main ways to ask hard questions and maintain rapport.

1   You can indicate a question in advance. For example, 'I would like to ask you a question about that…'

2   You can soften your questions either by voice tone or with qualifying phrases, for example:

'I would like to know whether...'
'I am interested to know if...'
'Would you mind telling me...'

Even a challenging question can be asked with respect and need not break rapport. Body language and voice tone are as important as the words. 'What do you want?' is an excellent basic coaching question, but asked in a sneering tone with a jabbing accusatory finger, it would completely break rapport.

Changing Emotional States

Questions can change a client's emotional state. They can put clients into unresourceful states either by poor use of voice tone and body language or by the limiting assumptions that could be built in. For example, 'What's the worst thing about this problem?' is a poor question because in order to understand the question the client has to go through a series of bad emotions, decide which is the worst and then answer. 'Just how hopeless do you feel?' is such a poor question that it would qualify as 'anti-coaching' – taking a client who is basically OK and making them feel worse after the coaching session.

Other questions, of course, will put the client in a resourceful state. Sometimes coaches will ask questions with the sole aim of doing this. These questions will be about:

the resources a client has
the people they love
the good experiences they have had

HOW TO ASK POWERFUL QUESTIONS

Questions are the main way in which the coach explores the client's issues and helps the client to resolve them. They can be very powerful. But powerful questions need to be precise.

Say, for example, the coach wants to ask a question to find out the value behind a goal. Here are three possible questions:

'If you get this goal, what will it get for you?'
'When you get this goal, what will it get for you?'
'When you get this goal, what will it mean to you?'

The first question introduces an element of doubt ('if') as to whether the client will get the goal. This is not a useful assumption. No one can know the future, but it is better to believe the client will be successful than to doubt them before they have even started.

The second question is the best because it presupposes the client will get the goal and focuses the client on what lies behind it.

The third question still presupposes the client will get the goal but is much less precise. The answer might be a mixture of values, beliefs, past experiences, associations and other outcomes. When you know exactly what you want to know, it is easier to word the question precisely.

Powerful coaching questions have five key characteristics.

1. They usually begin with the word 'what'.

'*What* do you want?', '*What* is important to you?' and '*What* could stop you achieving this goal?' are all examples of powerful questions. The first explores the client's goals, the second their values and the third any limiting beliefs or other obstructions that need to be overcome.

Questions that begin with the word 'why' are usually less powerful. These questions are usually enquiring about values, but a better question for values is '*What* is important to you about that?' 'Why is that important to you?' is not so precise because the client could answer with a description of other people's expectations or logical reasons as to why they took a certain course of action.

Likewise, 'Why did you do that?' could be interpreted as having an element of blame. The client might feel they were being called on to justify their action. Also, they might answer with logical reasons for their action or a description of the events that led up to their action rather than the values behind it or what they were trying to achieve by acting in that way.

There is one 'what' question that a client might ask you: 'What should I do?' 'Should' is a pressure word – it implies there is a rule that the client thinks they have to follow and they want you to tell them what it is. In effect they are saying 'Tell me what to do. Give me a rule to follow.' Resist the temptation to do this at all costs, even if what they should do seems crystal clear to you. The best reply to this question is another question: 'What do you want?' Once someone is clear about their own beliefs, values and goals they will know what to do.

2. Powerful questions lead to action.

They are solution-oriented. Intellectual understanding is not enough to solve a problem or get a goal. You have to *do* something about it.

3. Powerful questions are oriented towards goals rather than problems.

Coaching focuses on the present and future rather than the past. Rather than dwell on the problem, good coaching questions move the client on to a different and better future.

4. Powerful questions lead the client into the future rather than seek explanations in the past.

Powerful questions point the way forward. It is not necessary to understand exactly how a situation arose in order to solve it. If you are in the dark, you do not have to understand the theory of electricity in order to turn on an electric light switch.

5. Powerful questions contain powerful assumptions that are helpful for the client.

The basic structure of a good coaching question is:

What ... you ...verb ... future positive.

'What' makes it specific and goal-oriented.
'You' applies it to the client and makes the client accountable.
The verb means action.
The future positive leads the client towards the future they want.

This is not meant to be a formula that you apply rigidly. It is simply a useful basic structure around which you can be creative and improvise.
Here are some examples of powerful questions:

↓   'What do you want?'
     This is the basic question to discover goals.
↓   'What other choices do you have?'
     This question assumes the client has options.
↓   'What will this goal get for you?'
     This question gets the values behind the goal.
↓   'What is important to you about that?'
↓   This question will uncover values.
↓   What are you willing to give up to accomplish this?'
     This is a question about the ecology of the goal, the wider picture. Notice the language.
     The question assumes the client is willing and able to give something up. There is a huge

difference between this question and 'What will you have to lose to accomplish this?' Losing and giving up are not the same. When I lose something I may suffer. Giving up is voluntary.

↓ 'What are you unwilling to change?'

This is a more challenging question, and it assumes that change is possible and under the influence of the client.

↓ 'What were you trying to achieve when you did that?'

This is a good question if the client did something that did not turn out the way they expected. It focuses on outcomes and asks about the client's intention. The intention would have been good even if the result was bad. This is based on the NLP presupposition that every action is purposeful. It leads to the next powerful question:

↓ 'What can you learn from this?'

This is a good question when the client has made a mistake, in other words their intention did not match their behaviour or their efforts turned out badly. Rather than analyse the mistake, this question asks the client to look at it more dispassionately and learn from it.

↓ 'What will you do differently next time?'

This is the follow-up question to the last one.

↓ 'What is good about the present situation?'

This is a good question about ecology. It assumes that there are some good elements in the client's life at present that are worth keeping. This is an important question when you are working with goals. Every situation has a good side.

↓ 'What can you do to make a difference?'

This assumes that the client can make a difference.

↓ 'What could be stopping you from taking action?'

Again there is a focus on future action in this question. Do not ignore something that could stop the client from taking action.

Finally, four slightly different questions that can be useful as an ecology check:

↓ 'What is the worst thing that could happen if you did this?'

This looks to the future and asks the client to evaluate possible bad consequences. It can be useful if the future is uncertain, as the answer can show them that the outlook is not as bleak as they may have thought. It is also useful for 'downside planning'. If the client is prepared to cope with the worst possible contingency, then they can go forward with more confidence. Knowing that they can deal with the worst-case scenario will give them more confidence.

↓ 'What is the best thing that could happen if you did this?'

This is a good question for putting the client in a good state. Conversely, this question may make them realize the reward is not as great as they had thought. This can be a useful realization.

⬇   'What is the worst thing that could happen if you did not do this?'
This question forces the client to realize that not making a decision is actually a decision for the status quo and has consequences. Inaction is a choice. Doing nothing may make the situation worse.

⬇   'What is the best thing that could happen if you did not do this?'
This is a similar question, exploring the consequences of inaction.

These 'what' questions are immensely powerful.

There is also a place for questions beginning with 'how', but these are secondary. 'How' questions explore the means the client will use. They are primarily about the action plan, but you cannot formulate an action plan without having the goals and values first.

Questions beginning with 'when' are also useful, but you need to know 'what' and 'how' before you can decide 'when'.

So the overall sequence of questions in coaching is:

What (goals and values)
How (means of achievement)
When (time)

In the ebb and flow of the coaching session different questions will interweave like a beautiful tapestry as the coach and client work together to find answers. The language of questions will lead to new thinking that will lead to new actions. This is NLP coaching in action.

CHALLENGING QUESTIONS

Good questions get good information and often clarify exactly what a client means. Questions can also be used to challenge a client's self-imposed limits and to open up options. To do this, a coach needs to listen carefully behind the words to the thinking that the words imply. When a client uses a form of words that limits their choices, it shows that they are thinking in a limiting way, because language reflects thought. If their thinking is limited, that means that their choice of action is limited. Therefore NLP can open up the path to action through challenging the words the client uses.

Words   *Thinking*   *Action*
Challenge the words ... to free the thinking ... to take action

There are several patterns of language that a good coach needs to listen for. They may then choose to challenge these patterns immediately or wait until later, perhaps linking up that information with other problems the client has.

Unconsidered Opinions

We all have opinions, but these can be limiting in two situations.

First the client may state their opinions as if they were facts. But opinions are based on beliefs and these beliefs may be mistaken. Yet from these opinions we judge ourselves and others.

Secondly, clients may give other people's opinions as if they were their own. So they may judge themselves and others not by their own values, but by the values of others, perhaps their parents, friends, peers or significant figures in their childhood. These judgements may be well out of date, but the client has not yet realized that they have gone stale because they have never really examined them. Judgements and opinions that the client does not own can cause trouble. By pointing them out, the coach allows the client to evaluate them.

Another class of judgements that the coach needs to listen for are comparisons. Listen carefully when the client uses words like 'better', 'worse', 'bad', 'good' or 'easier'. Comparisons may be limiting the client's life if they are based on unsuitable or unrealistic comparisons. A client may be depressed or demotivated if they compare themselves to an impossible standard or unrealistic role model (which may come from significant childhood figures) and feel inadequate without ever realizing why. The coach can challenge the unrealistic standard of comparison and give them a better one.

Some clients are still trying to live up to parental standards and feel inadequate as adults. It is more empowering (and realistic) for the client to compare themselves to where they were some months ago than to some impractical standard. Clients learn to set their own standards in the coaching process.

Adverbs like 'obviously', 'clearly', 'of course' and 'definitely' also always show judgements. Listen carefully whenever the client says 'Clearly this is so…' or 'Obviously this is so…' It may be clear and obvious to the client, but that does not make it true.

Make sure the client owns their judgements and makes realistic comparisons.

Overgeneralizations

We learn by generalizing – we encounter one or two examples of something and conclude that everything in the same class operates in the same way. Very often, we are right. We learn to drive one car and then are able to drive other cars. We do not have to learn to drive anew with every different car we drive. This is how we build habits – they make things easier.

The problem comes when we generalize from a few examples that are not representative. Listen carefully when a client uses words like 'always', 'never', 'everybody' or 'nobody' – words that imply there are no exceptions. These kinds of words are limiting because you have assumed that everything is the same, you have made a generalization.

When you hear a client making a generalization, especially if it is used to back up a problem, challenge it. Ask the client to consider whether their statement really has no exceptions. If they say something like 'I always get that wrong' you can say '*Always*? Has there never been any time in your life when you did not get that wrong?' Even one exception will disprove the generalization. When a client overgeneralizes, it is often a useful clue that there is a limiting belief behind the language.

Unwarranted Assumptions

These work in exactly the same way as the assumptions or presuppositions behind questions. What has to be true for you to accept what the client says? Is the client drawing you into their problem? Often clients make assumptions and build them into their language in such a way that you accept them in order to deal with their issue. However, often the assumption *is* the issue. For example, a client says, 'I want to work on how my husband's moods make me depressed.' This assumes the husband's moods are the cause of the depression. They could be an important factor, but not the most important one.

Listen for limiting assumptions, for example (the assumption is in brackets):

'How many times must I tell them before they will stop it?' (I will have to tell them a number of times before they will stop.)
'When are they going to act responsibly?' (They are not acting responsibly now.)
'How bad can this get?' (It's bad now and will get worse.)
'I am not sure whether I can mend my ways.' (My ways are broken.)
'How badly does he want to hurt me?' (He wants to hurt me.)

Presuppositions are often cunningly disguised as 'why' questions, for example:

'Why is he so ungrateful?' (He is ungrateful.)
'Why can't she do anything right?' (She does nothing right.)
'Why am I so insensitive?' (I am insensitive.)

Assumptions also may be hidden in behind words like 'when' and 'since' and 'if', for example:

'When is he going to realize that I don't like that?' (I don't like that and he hasn't realized yet.)

Mind Reading

One source of assumptions is mind reading. A client may assume they know what another person is thinking with little evidence. They assume they know the intention when all they see is the behaviour. Behaviour is visible, but intention is invisible.

When a client mind reads, it is always worth questioning whether their mind reading is accurate. They could be right, but they could be wrong. Ask them how they know that the person is thinking the way that they are thinking. They may be right, but why not be sure?

In the same way, some clients assume that other people should know what they want and ought to act on it. This is mind reading in reverse – they assume other people can mind read them, and they may get upset if other people don't meet their needs, even though they have never made them clear. Clients who habitually mind read in reverse will be very dissatisfied and often angry with other people. They think others are deliberately thwarting them.

Pressure Words

'Should' and 'shouldn't', 'must' and 'mustn't', 'ought' and 'oughtn't' are all examples of pressure words. They create pressure to do or refrain from doing something. They imply a rule, and often the client is not aware of the rule.

Some examples:

'I *should* do better.'
'I *must* finish that by the end of the month.'
'I *mustn't* make a mistake.'
'They *shouldn't* do that.'

As a coach, you can challenge these pressure words in three different ways.

↓ You can challenge the consequences of the rule in the client's mind by asking what would happen if the rule were broken. If the client says 'I *should* do that', you can ask 'What would happen if you did not?' or 'Why not?' (The latter question demands some degree of rapport.)

↓ You can also challenge the tyranny of the 'should' by saying something like 'Just suppose for a moment that you don't. What would that be like?' If the client says 'I *should not* do that' then you can challenge by saying 'What would happen if you did?' or perhaps 'Who says so?'

↓ You can also suggest other alternatives by saying 'Just suppose you could… What would that be like…?'

Pressure words may have a basis in accepted practice or morality, but if you listen, you will be surprised how often clients use them to compel themselves to do or not do all sorts of things that do not matter. These pressure words may also point towards limiting beliefs. Catch every single pressure word you hear.

Turning Pressure into Purpose

You can turn pressure into purpose by shifting the client's focus to their goals.

Ask the client to turn their 'shoulds', 'oughts', 'musts' and 'need tos' into 'I want to…' And ask them to say this out loud. So if the client says something like '*I should* visit my parents', ask them to say '*I want to* visit my parents' and then ask them how that feels. Often, the client will feel they do not *want* to do this; it is not in line with their goals. So why then are they saying they should do it? What rule are they applying to themselves? They may feel guilty, and behind the guilt there is likely to be resentment.

In the same way, if they say something like, '*I should not* do this', ask them to say out loud, '*I do not want* to do this.' Again, ask them how they feel when they do this. This pattern puts the client in control of their action, gives them a choice and turns their attention back to their goals.

When a client says they 'can't' do something, explore that statement as a belief. The obstacle may be in their own minds and not in reality.

There are many ways to challenge a client who says they cannot do something. For example, a client may say something like 'I just can't relax.' You can challenge this in a number of ways:

1   You can treat it like a pressure word and challenge the imagined consequences by asking: 'What would happen if you did?'
2   You can ask: 'What stops you?' This question contains the assumption that the client can relax, only something is preventing them from doing so.
3   You can ask the client to make the distinction between possibility and capability by asking: 'Cannot, or don't know how to?' Sometimes clients think something is impossible when in fact they just do not know how to do it – they confuse possibility with capability. They only need to learn how to.

'But…'

Listen for the word 'but' in the client's language. 'But' is a word that immediately qualifies or even negates what has gone before. When you hear 'but' ask them to replace it with 'and'. For example, instead of 'I agree with you, *but* I think you should also consider this point', ask them to say, 'I agree with you, *and* I think you should also consider this point.' This links the two together and is more likely to be received with an open mind.

Another way you can deal with 'but' is to switch the order of the two statements. So if a client says something like 'I will try to do it, but it will be difficult', ask them to say instead 'It will be difficult, but I will try to do it.' This simple change makes a big difference.

Sometimes the word 'but' conceals what might be called an 'aside'. An aside is a throwaway comment that is said as if it were trivial, but is really a crucial issue. The coach needs to be alert to pick up these asides and start to question them. They are important *and* the client is trying to slide over them quickly.

Some clients will constantly use the phrase 'yes, but'. Nothing the coach suggests will quite work, there is always a 'but'. This can be a frustrating pattern for the coach to deal with. 'Yes, but' shows the client is mismatching all the time. They are always looking for exceptions and difficulties. Focus them on the difficulty that this pattern is causing them. Give them the task of cutting this pattern from their vocabulary for a week. Ask permission to challenge them every time you hear them say it. Ask them to replace the pattern with another phrase such as 'I have a concern about that…'

Meanings

We all make meaning of our experience. Intellectually we know that we do not control the world, but we do take many things personally when they have no connection to us. Wisdom is not so much about what happens to us as about the meaning we make of our experiences. Listen for how the client interprets what happens to them. Some clients connect a series of events in ways that make them feel bad or back up their limiting beliefs. In particular, listen for how clients back up their interpretations, for example 'He was late *so* he didn't care about the meeting.' Here, the client is saying that being late means he didn't care.

Another example would be if a client were making a presentation and someone in the audience yawned. The client might take this to mean that the person was bored and therefore their presentation was not interesting. Further, they might generalize and believe that they are not good at addressing an audience … ever.

Someone else making a presentation might conclude that a yawn meant that person was tired. Maybe they had a late night and maybe it would be a good idea to give everyone a short break, so they could pay better attention. This person would draw no conclusions from the yawn about how good they were as a speaker and certainly not form the belief that they were not good at addressing an audience. Same experience but very different meaning. When you do not know the answer, one interpretation is just as realistic as the other.

Abstract Language

Finally, listen for a lot of abstract language. Abstract nouns are those like 'stress', 'relationship', 'failure' and 'depression'. Abstract nouns take a lot of detail away. There is no sense of action – an abstract noun has no doer and no action. Abstractions are the enemies of action-based coaching.

> **Do this experiment.**
> ↓ **Say to yourself, 'Communication is important.' Notice what thoughts come to your mind. Your pictures may be abstract and still.**
> ↓ **Now say this to yourself, 'I want to communicate.' Notice the feeling of activity this brings with it. You are doing something rather than contemplating something.**

Abstract nouns are useful and sometimes necessary, but the coach should make sure that the client does not use them habitually, because this could show there is no change in their experience.

'My communication in this relationship gives me a lot of stress and fear' contains four abstractions ('communication', 'relationship', 'stress' and 'fear'). No coach should let a client get away with a sentence like that. Instead they should start to probe into how the client is communicating, how are they relating, how they are being stressed and what they are frightened of. Put the actor into the abstraction and bring it to life.

Abstractions like 'communication' are nouns, but what they describe are really processes. When a client says they have a lot of stress, it sounds as though stress is some discrete entity, but it is not, it is something that is happening, so the coach needs to ask questions like:

'How are you feeling that stress?'
'How exactly are you being stressed?'
'What is stressing you?'

If the client says they have a fear, then the coach should ask what they are frightened of. When the client says that communication is bad, the coach needs to ask *who* is communicating, *what* they are communicating about and *how* it is going wrong.

Many of the powerful questions will make it difficult for the client to reply using abstract language. When the coach turns frozen abstractions into verbs it puts the client into the picture as an agent who has choice and can take action.

Many of these language patterns point to limiting beliefs. Limiting beliefs are often our biggest obstacles. Empowering beliefs can become our greatest resources. The next chapter is devoted to beliefs.

SUMMARY

Coaching has a structure.
It begins with rapport and explores the client's goals, values and beliefs.
The coach gives the client tasks and supports them in carrying them out, so the client can re-evaluate their habits.

Questions are the main way in which a coach helps a client.
Coaching questions:

↓ *are irresistible invitations to think*
↓ *have a purpose*
↓ *focus like a spotlight on the client's experience*
↓ *light up some areas of the client's experience and put others in shadow*
↓ *contain assumptions*
↓ *have an honest intention and ask for an honest answer*
↓ *need good timing*
↓ *gather good information*
↓ *build and maintain rapport*
↓ *elicit emotional states from the client*

Powerful questions have the following attributes:

They usually begin with the word 'what'.
They lead to action.
They are goal-oriented, not problem-oriented.
They focus on the present and the future, not the past.
They contain empowering assumptions.
They have a defined purpose.

The basic structure of a good coaching question is:

What ... you ... verb ... future positive.

'What' questions focus on goals and values.
'How' questions focus on ways of achieving the client's goals.
'When' questions focus on the timing.

The coach uses a different kind of question to challenge the client when they use language that shows that their thinking is limited. Coaches challenge the language in order to challenge the thinking behind it to free the client for action and give them more choice.

Challenge a client when they have:
> *unconsidered opinions*

and make:
> *unsuitable comparisons*
>
> *overgeneralizations*
>
> *unwarranted assumptions*
>
> *inappropriate interpretations*

and form:
> *abstractions*

and perform:
> *mind reading*

Ask the client to replace 'but' with 'and'.

Turn pressure words such as 'I should...' and 'I must...' into purpose by replacing them with 'I can...'or, 'I want...'

ACTION STEPS

If you want to understand, act. Here are some ways to explore the ideas in this chapter. You can also use them as tasks for your client and yourself if you wish.

1 Notice what questions you ask when you are working with clients. Experiment by rephrasing your questions so they begin with the word 'what'. What difference does this make to the quality of the answers that you get?

2 Reserve 10 minutes in one session with a client where you only ask questions. Do nothing else but ask questions (unless this is completely inappropriate). What effect does this have? How easy is it for you?

3 Listen throughout one day for people making generalizations, for example 'never', 'always', 'everybody', 'nobody'. Do not challenge them, but how many of these examples do you think are literally true and have absolutely no counter-examples?

4 Spend another day listening for pressure words *in your own speech*, for example 'I should...', 'I must...', 'I ought to...' When you hear yourself using any of these words, mentally say the sentence again, but replace the pressure words with 'I can...'or, 'I want to...' What difference does this make?

5   What questions would you really want to answer? Formulate them. For example:

'How can I help my children to be happy and successful?'

'How can I have good health?'

'What does death mean?'

'How can I be my best?'

What do these questions say about you as a person?

CHAPTER 7

BELIEFS: THE RULES OF YOUR LIFE

⇨ ⇨ ⇨ Beliefs are the rules of your life, the rules you live by. These rules may be liberating and empowering and give you permission to get your goals and live your values. They may also be obstructions, making goals impossible or leading you to believe you are not capable of getting them.

Beliefs are principles of action, not empty theories. So if you want to know what a person believes, notice what they *do*, not what they say they believe. We believe in gravity and act as if it exists. We do not try to test it by trying to walk on air. Gravity does not seem to be influenced one way or the other by our belief in it. However, our relationships, abilities and possibilities are influenced by our beliefs about them.

We form our beliefs as the result of our experiences. Then we act as if they are true. In one sense, they are self-fulfilling prophecies. If you believe you are a likeable person, you will act that way, approach people openly, be gregarious and enjoy being with people. They will warm to you and so confirm your belief. We think that beliefs are formed by experiences, but equally experiences are the result of beliefs.

This means you can choose your beliefs. If you like the results you get, then keep acting that way and keep your beliefs. If you don't like the results, act another way and change your beliefs.

Beliefs can and do change. But the belief that beliefs are changeable is in itself a challenging belief to many people because they tend to think of beliefs as possessions. People talk about 'having' and 'holding' beliefs, 'losing' or 'gaining' them. No one wants to 'lose' something. It would be better talking about 'leaving' or 'outgrowing' beliefs, rather than 'losing' them.

Also, we have a personal investment in our beliefs. When the world confirms them, then it makes sense to us, is predictable and gives us a sense of security and certainty. We even may take a perverse pleasure in disaster, providing we have predicted it. 'I told you so' is a satisfying phrase, not because we wanted anything to go wrong, but because our beliefs were proved right.

COACHING WITH BELIEFS

Some coaching can take place without dealing with beliefs. When a client comes to a coach to improve or gain a skill, they may already believe that they can do it. Likewise, if a client comes with a business or personal problem, the coach may help them find a solution within the framework of their existing beliefs. This is 'single loop coaching' because the coach helps the client get their goal by clarifying the goal, helping them to take action and get good feedback, and learn in the process.

Single loop coaching

However, if the client has doubts about their ability to get their goal, then the coach needs to explore their beliefs.

Coaching that deals with beliefs is more powerful because it not only solves the problem but also changes the thinking that led to the problem in the first place. This is 'double loop coaching' because it brings the client's belief into the feedback loop. And because beliefs act as pervasive rules about what is possible, the client will also become more creative in other areas of their life.

Here, the client learns that their beliefs about the problem are part of the problem. By changing beliefs, they come to take new actions that not only solve the problem but lead to new experiences outside the context of the problem.

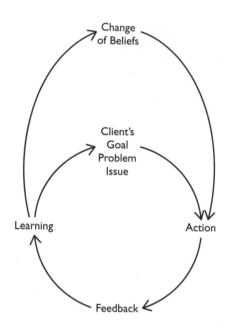

Double loop coaching

One way you can start to work with a client on beliefs is to give them the 'Beliefs in Time' worksheet (*see Resources, page 193*). This explores beliefs at different ages about age, beauty, happiness, home, love, career and possibilities. For example, what did you believe about age when you were a child? Most likely you divided the world into children, who were about your age, and grown ups, who were older. Then in your teens, there were children, your peers and old people (maybe very old people). As you entered your twenties the category 'being old' may have tended to recede, like the hairline, to later and later in life. What did you believe about love when you were a child? And when you were a teenager? And in your twenties? This worksheet is very revealing and it makes the point that beliefs do change. They may change as a result of a powerful experience or may evolve naturally.

When talking about positive beliefs with a client, check whether they express the client at the identity level. For example, one client may say 'I want to have happiness.' Another client may say 'I want to be happy.' Even though these sound the same, the inner meaning is different. Everything that you *have* is not *you*, it belongs somewhere outside you and is not part of who you are. This means that you can 'have' something today, but it is possible to lose it tomorrow. Much better to live it as part of who you are.

In some languages, like Portuguese, there are two verbs for the English verb 'to be.' One implies permanence, that something is part of a person's existence. In Portuguese, this verb is *ser*. The other verb describes something that is temporary and is more about the actual state of mind and body at the moment. In Portuguese that verb is *estar*. So when I say 'I am tired', I am referring to a temporary state of the body and even the mind, so I say, '*Eu estou cansada*,' using the verb estar. But if I say 'I am Andrea', this is permanent, so I use the verb *ser*: '*Eu sou Andrea.*' I can be tired sometimes, but I am always Andrea. When I am tired I do not lose my identity, it is a temporary state, I am not a tired person. And I can say 'I am happy!' It doesn't matter if I feel sad sometimes, I am a happy person.

English does not make this distinction in the verb 'to be', but the coach should make it. Sometimes clients generalize from temporary states or beliefs and attach them to their identity; they are misled by language. Temporary negative beliefs are much easier to deal with. Here is a useful rule for the coach to follow:

Any negative belief, make temporary. Any empowering belief, make permanent.

Teach the client the distinction between the two, even if their language does not carry it.

EMPOWERING BELIEFS

Coaching acts from empowering beliefs. Here are some of the presuppositions of coaching. Act as if these are true and you will be an excellent coach.

↓ If you want to understand, act.
   The first principle of coaching is that the learning is in the doing. Change comes from action, not from intellectual understanding. Action results in feedback and learning. Action in coaching is moving towards your goals, living your values and testing your beliefs about yourself and others.

↓ There is no failure, only feedback.
   Failure is only a judgement about short-term results. If you have not reached your goal, all it means is that you have not reached your goal *yet*. Failure is not a sensible idea because you cannot prove a negative. You cannot say you have failed unless you give up, and that is your choice.

↓ We already have all the resources we need or can create them.
   There are no unresourceful people, only unresourceful states of mind. The coach works to bring out the client's inner resources. Our deeper wisdom is waiting to be discovered.

↓ All behaviour has a purpose.
   Our actions are not random; we are always trying to achieve something. We are always moving towards some sort of goal, although we may not be aware of it. Set your own goals, because if you do not, there are many people who will happily set them for you.

↓   Having a choice is better than having no choice.

If you give a client a better choice according to their values and beliefs, then they will take it.

↓   You are doing the best you can and you can probably do better.

↓   You create your own reality.

We all have different experiences, interests, moods, commitments, likes, dislikes and preoccupations. So we form different beliefs from our life experiences, we pursue different goals and have different values. These goals, beliefs and values are the main features of our mental maps, which shape the world we perceive. We act as if these mental maps are real. Our mental maps may be good ones, allowing a lot of freedom to explore, or they may be limited, with tight boundaries, hedged with seeming dangers. The coach has their own map and they respect and work with the client's worldview. The intention is not to bring the client's worldview in line with the coach's, but to give them more choices in their world.

↓   Coaching is an equal, synergistic partnership.

↓   Relationships are more than the sum of their parts.

If you think one and one only make two, it is only because you have forgotten the power of the 'and' – the power of the connection.

↓   The client has the answers.

The coach has the questions.

These presuppositions can become valuable coaching resources. Say a client is having difficulties in their relationship with their partner. If only their partner would stop behaving in a certain way, then everything would be OK. They think their partner is being unreasonable. What can a coach do?

First they can carefully observe the client, listen to their voice tone, calibrate the client. Then they can ask the client to choose one of these powerful presuppositions or ask the client to think of a powerful idea of their own and imagine that it was true in this situation. Suppose the presupposition the client picked was 'You are doing the best you can.' The coach would ask the client to imagine for a moment that this is true in that situation with their partner. What is that like? How do they feel? How would they think differently?

In this example, the client would probably stop blaming themselves for the bad relationship – they would realize they were doing their best. Secondly, they would realize that their partner was also doing their best, given their map of reality. And if they were given a better choice, they would take it.

Now the client has shifted from wanting to make a change in their partner to changing their thinking about the situation and seeing it from their partner's point of view as well as their own.

The coach would calibrate the client while they thought about the belief. They would be likely to speak and act very differently from before. The client does not have to think that the belief that brought about the change is always true, only apply it in that situation.

Finally the coach could give the client a task. The next time they begin a quarrel with their partner they are to remember that belief, act as if it were true and see what the result is. Will it be different from the usual result? Almost certainly yes.

In the next session, coach and client can discuss the difference and what the client learned from the situation.

Here's a summary of the process.

Coaching Intervention: Using Powerful Beliefs

↓ Calibrate the client when they talk about the situation.
How do they look?
How do they sound?

↓ What words are they using?
Ask the client to pick one of the coaching presuppositions or an empowering belief that they know and respect. What belief do they intuitively think would help in that situation?

↓ Ask the client to imagine that the belief is true. Either they can imagine what it would be like if that belief were true or think of a time when it was true for them. Calibrate the client.

↓ Ask the client to imagine the original problem situation again, but this time with the new belief. How would they act differently? How would they see the other person differently? Calibrate the client again. Make sure that they keep the physiology associated with the empowering belief.

↓ When the client reports a helpful difference as a result of the presupposition and you can confirm this with your calibration, give them the task of using that presupposition the next time the situation arises.

↓ Together you can discuss the result at the next coaching session.

LIMITING BELIEFS

Limiting beliefs are the major culprits stopping us achieving our goals and living our values. They act as rules that stop us getting what is possible, what we are capable of and what we deserve. When a coach asks, 'What stops you from achieving your goal?' the answers very often are limiting beliefs.

Limiting beliefs may come from childhood when we copied our parents – parents are never perfect. These early beliefs often stay hidden and we do not consciously evaluate them as adults. We also pick up limiting beliefs from the media. Soap operas set up situations where the characters have to act out stupid limitations, otherwise there is no drama.

Here are some typical limiting beliefs:

'I need to work very hard to have enough money to live.'
'No pain – no gain.'
'I need to be rich to be happy.'
'Success takes a long time.'
'I can't trust anybody.'
'Most people are luckier than me.'
'You can't get over a bad start in life.'
'I can't work a computer.'
'I can't live without that work.'
'I can't win without other people losing.'
'I never get what I want.'
'Other people are better than me.'
'Coaching is difficult.'
'I am not a flexible person.'
'I do not deserve to succeed.'
'I can't get what I want.'
'I have reached my limits.'

These and similar beliefs are only true if you act as if they are. Suppose they are mistaken: what difference would that make? Is the difference worthwhile?

Identifying Limiting Beliefs

In coaching, sometimes simply being able to articulate limiting beliefs and seeing their effect is enough for a client to change their beliefs and therefore their reality.

People are not usually aware of their limiting beliefs. *The first step is to put them into language.* Then they are in the open and can be examined. There are two simple ways to do this. The first is the 'Limiting Beliefs' worksheet.

Identifying Limiting Beliefs Worksheet

↓   Ask the client to think about an important goal.
↓   Ask them, while keeping that goal in mind, to say *out loud*, each of the following sentences. In each case ask them to state their actual goal

when the sentence says 'my goal'. So, if the goal is to have better relationships, the first statement they make is, 'I deserve to have better relationships.'

↓   As they do so, both you and the client should give a score from one to ten. One means that they do not believe the statement, and ten means that they completely believe the statement.

1   'I deserve to achieve [my goal].'
    1   2   3   4   5   6   7   8   9   10
    Do not believe   Completely believe

2   'I have the skills and abilities necessary to achieve [my goal].'
    1   2   3   4   5   6   7   8   9   10
    Do not believe   Completely believe

3   'It is possible to achieve [my goal].'
    1   2   3   4   5   6   7   8   9   10
    Do not believe   Completely believe

4   '[My goal] is clear.'
    1   2   3   4   5   6   7   8   9   10
    Do not believe   Completely believe

5   '[My goal] is desirable.'
    1   2   3   4   5   6   7   8   9   10
    Do not believe   Completely believe

6   '[My goal] is ecological.'
    1   2   3   4   5   6   7   8   9   10
    Do not believe   Completely believe

7   '[My goal] is worthwhile.'
    1   2   3   4   5   6   7   8   9   10
    Do not believe   Completely believe

This can be very revealing. Low scores (less than seven) show a limiting belief or that the person has not thought about the goal sufficiently. The coach needs to probe: 'Why are you doubtful?' 'What could be making you doubt this?'

As a coach, do you give the statement the same score as the client? For example, if a client says, 'I deserve to achieve my goal' and you pick up some doubt in their voice tone and body language, you may score it as a seven. The client, however, scores it as a ten. Challenge them: 'Are you sure?'

Remember that you are doing this in the service of the client's best self. Sometimes clients score what they would like to believe rather than what they really believe. Make sure you are satisfied that the client is congruent and honest in their assessment.

The second way to identify limiting beliefs is by asking the client why they are not achieving their goal. What do they think is stopping them? The answers show what they perceive as limits. Often these limits are more about the client than about the world.

A good principle to work from is:

Whatever the client says is stopping them from getting their goal is a belief and comes from the client, not reality.

Obstructions are created on the outside world from limiting beliefs in the client's mind.

The PAW Process

In order to achieve their goals clients need to believe three things:

Possibility   It is possible to achieve them.
Ability   They are capable of achieving them.
Worthiness   They deserve to achieve them.

Possibility, Ability and Worthiness are the three keys to achievement – the PAW Process.

Possibility

First a client has to believe that their goals are possible – for them. Otherwise, they will not even try to achieve them.

We all have physical limits because we are human, not superheroes. However:

We do not know what these limits are.
We cannot know what they are until we reach them.

Often we mistake possibility for competence. We think something is not possible when in fact we just do not know *how* to do it.

Ability

When a client believes that their goal is possible, then at least they are in the game. The next block is that they believe they are incapable of getting their goal. They have put a mental ceiling on their achievement.

A coach can give their clients one basic true belief:

You have not yet reached the limit of what you are capable of.

The only way you can prove you are capable of achieving a goal is when you achieve it. Until then you do not know, so it is better to believe that you can. It is just as realistic to believe you can as to believe you cannot. You can never prove you cannot achieve a goal because you cannot prove a negative. You can only say that you have not achieved it *yet*.

Once it was thought impossible for any human being to run a mile in less than four minutes, then Roger Bannister did it at Oxford on 6 May 1954. After that a strange thing happened – more and more athletes started running a mile in under four minutes and dozens had done it, two years on. This 'impossible' achievement is now commonplace. Bannister's achievement changed a worldwide belief in what was possible.

So ask the client to keep an open mind about their ability.

Sometimes clients will cheerfully announce that they do not have the ability to do something. They may even boast of their limitations, mistaking this for modesty. Listen for a day or two and you will hear a string of admissions from people about what they cannot do:

'I am no good with money.'
'I can't control my diet.'
'I just can't arrive on time for anything.'

When you hear this sort of thing from a client, ask them to change their language, for example:

'I am not good with money *at the moment*.'
'*I do not believe* I am any good with money.'
'I am not controlling my eating habits *at the moment*.'
'In the past, *I have not* arrived on time for appointments.'

Changing the language is the first step to changing the thinking and hence the beliefs.

A good task for a client who is too free with admissions of incompetence is for them to stop making those admissions. This does not mean that they have to say they are good at these things, or even announce that they can do them at all. They simply have to stop saying that they cannot do them. They may feel uncomfortable at first, but this is the first step towards becoming more realistic about their abilities.

The trouble with public announcements of incompetence is that other people believe them. They do not expect you to succeed, so they do not encourage you or challenge you. They reinforce your belief.

Another pattern you may find with clients is that they give excuses in advance. They tell you why they are going to fail or plead extenuating circumstances in advance. Usually if a client comes up with an excuse beforehand it is because they feel they are going to need it. They are setting themselves up for failure. There may be some very good reasons why they do not achieve particular goals, for example, they may have a cold at a crucial presentation and not be able to think (or speak) as clearly as they would like. Even so, it is good not to make the excuse beforehand. Having a prior excuse makes it easier to fail.

Worthiness

Finally, the client must believe they deserve to achieve their goals. Often there is a belief left over from childhood that they do not deserve anything that they have not worked hard for. Or the belief may be that they only get things because of others' generosity, not for themselves. Some clients believe that others have to fail for them to succeed and this makes them incongruent about success.

A task for clients in this situation could be to re-evaluate their childhood from the point of view that they do deserve things, but others do not think they do – the belief is in others. Sometimes they may need to speak to their parents.

Some of the most valuable coaching is getting clients to feel they deserve things – they deserve to have the feelings they have, they deserve to get the goals they want.

This can lead to some deep conversations that may lead clients ro re-evaluate their life. Cultural beliefs also play a part. For example in Northern Europe, it is a common belief that if you do not have to work hard for something, then you do not deserve it. This is a sophisticated version of the belief, 'No pain no gain.' It is simply not true, because in other cultures, notably some Latin cultures, the opposite idea is prevalent, that is, if a goal takes a lot of effort, then you shouldn't really have it. You can start to shake these sorts of beliefs by asking questions like:

'What would have to happen for you to deserve it?'

'Under what circumstances would you deserve it?'

'Do you know anyone you think would deserve it?'

The PAW Process Exercise

This is a powerful process you can use with your clients to deal with their limiting beliefs.

↓ Ask them to explore one of their important goals with the 'Limiting Beliefs' worksheet (*page 101*). They will find some limiting beliefs in the areas of possibility, capability or worthiness.

↓ Make sure they really do want the goal and check the ecology. Is it really good for them? Does it fit their values? Does it hurt significant other people in their life?

↓ Ask them what stops them from achieving their goal.
Treat the obstacles they come up with as beliefs, not reality.
These obstacles usually fall into five categories:

> They don't have the resources – people, equipment, time.
> They have the resources, but they don't know what to do.
> They know what to do, but they do not believe they have the skill to do it.
> They have the skill, but it doesn't seem worth it.
> It is worthwhile, but they do not deserve it or it does not seem right at a deep level.

↓ Ask them to think about the limiting beliefs they have discovered.

> Which ones are they certain about?
> Which ones are they uncertain about?
> Which beliefs are important to obtaining this goal?
> Which, to their mind, are the most important obstacles?
> Which ones are not important?

They can plot this on the Beliefs Grid (*see Resources, page 192*). Beliefs that they are certain about and are important to achieving the goal will go in the upper left corner. Beliefs that they are uncertain about but are important go in the bottom left corner. Beliefs that they are certain about but are not important go in the upper right corner. Beliefs that they are uncertain about but are not important go in the bottom right corner.

↓ Ask the client to pick a belief that is important – one on the left-hand side of the grid. Between you, construct a task for them that will test this belief. You are not trying to prove this belief wrong, but to get feedback on it. Limiting beliefs grow and proliferate in the dark if they never get the light of feedback from the outside world. This is not a process for changing beliefs, but for dragging them into the light of feedback. The client has made their belief true by acting it out. With feedback, the belief will be weakened and the client will often drop it spontaneously.

BELIEF CHANGE

Beliefs do change naturally through life, as the Beliefs in Time worksheet (*see Resources, page 193*) demonstrates. The cycle goes like this:

↓   dissatisfaction with current events
↓   doubting the existing belief
↓   wanting to believe something different
↓   a new belief
↓   the old belief joins the group of outmoded beliefs

If you want to change a client's beliefs, here is a process which utilizes what happens naturally.

Belief Change Process

↓   **Identify the limiting belief that the client wants to shift.**
> Ask the client to write it down in precise words. Once a belief is identified in words, it has lost half its power, it is vulnerable.
> Find out the positive intention of this belief. What does it achieve for the client that is positive, despite the fact that it is limiting in a number of ways?

↓   **Ask the client what they would rather believe.**
This new belief should have the following characteristics:
> It should be stated in the positive (i.e. it should not contain any negative words like 'no' or 'not' or 'never' or 'none').
> It should be open to feedback and so able to be tested against experience.
> It should be ecological (i.e. they should feel comfortable about it and believe it will not harm their relationships with other people).
> It should fulfil the same positive intention as the old belief.

↓   **Ask the client to write down this new belief. It needs to be carefully phrased – it should be about self-development and it should be worded in the present tense *as if it is occurring now*. For example, if your goal were to increase your self-confidence, a suitable new belief would be:**

'I am believing in myself and my abilities more and more.'

This makes it relevant now and gives it direction and energy. Do not phrase a belief as if it has already happened.

↓ What is it like to doubt a belief?

Get the client to remember a time when they doubted a former belief. The Beliefs in Time worksheet (*page 193*) is a perfect preparation. Then ask them to think about their old limiting belief while in that state of doubt.

As they do this, start to undermine the belief by asking them:

'What are the drawbacks of this old belief?'

'Does it really fit in with what is important to you?' (This appeals to the client's values.)

'Has there ever been a time when what happened did not bear out this belief?' (This asks the client to find a counter-example.)

'What was it like to believe this old belief?' (This gets the client to think about the belief through time, not just now.)

After this, distract them from their state of being open to doubt. This is known as a 'break state'. When clients are strongly in a state and you want to bring them back to themselves, distract them in some way, maybe with a joke or by getting them to get up and move around.

↓ What it is like to be open to belief?

Ask the client to think of a time when they were open to a new belief. Again the Beliefs in Time worksheet could provide an example.

Have the client think about their new belief while in this state.

'How does it feel?'

'How is it a better choice than the old belief?'

'How well does it meet the positive intention of the old belief?'

'What would it be like to believe this?'

'What difference would it make?'

'What could you do that you cannot currently do?'

'What would you stop doing that you currently do?'

↓ Ask the client to evaluate both the old and the new beliefs.

Do they need to refine the new belief?

Are there any 'yes, buts'?

How is the new belief more useful than the old belief?

↓ Ask the client to move the old belief to a 'Museum of Old Beliefs' (where it will be available again, should they ever want it).

↓ Action! What will they do differently as a result of the new belief? Give them a task immediately, based on this new belief being true for them now.

Changing beliefs is a powerful intervention and can open the way for a major change in the client's experience and a swift progress towards their goals. The next chapter focuses on more NLP interventions in the coaching process.

SUMMARY

Beliefs are rules about life. They may be empowering or they may be limiting.
They are principles of action and we act as if they are true.
We can believe in anything we want.

Our beliefs influence our experiences. They make some experiences possible and others impossible. Each of us has a reality created and backed up by our beliefs. We act according to that reality.
Beliefs change as a result of experience, sometimes gradually and sometimes abruptly.
You can tell what a person believes by how they act, not what they say.
Single loop coaching is when the client does not change any of their beliefs (and does not need to).
Double loop coaching makes the client question and change their beliefs.

The beliefs of coaching are:

↓ *If you want to understand, act.*
↓ *There is no failure, only feedback.*
↓ *We already have all the resources we need or can create them.*
↓ *All behaviour has a purpose.*
↓ *Having a choice is better than having no choice.*
↓ *You are doing the best you can.*
↓ *You create your own reality.*
↓ *Coaching is an equal, synergistic partnership.*
↓ *The client has the answers.*

The first step in dealing with limiting beliefs is to put them into words.
Limiting beliefs usually fall into three categories:
  Possibility: We think the goal is impossible.
  Ability: We think we are not capable of achieving it.
  Worth: We think we do not deserve to achieve it.
Believing in possibility, ability and worth is the key to achievement.
We cannot know the limits of what is possible for us until we reach them.
It is impossible to prove you cannot do something or that something is impossible.

Do not publicly say what you believe are your limitations.
Do not make excuses for failure in advance.

Beliefs change naturally through life. The process is:

↓ *dissatisfaction with current events*
↓ *doubting the existing belief*
↓ *wanting to believe something different*
↓ *a new belief*
↓ *the old belief joins the group of outmoded beliefs*

Coaching uses this natural process to change limiting beliefs.

ACTION STEPS

If you want to understand, act. Here are some ways to explore the ideas in this chapter. You can also use them as tasks for your client and yourself if you wish.

1   When you make a decision, on what do you base it? Facts? Your experience? Other people's opinions? Often we form beliefs and make decisions on the basis of what other people say, what we read on the internet or in newspapers, or see on television. They may be good sources, but it is still second-hand experience. What have these sources done to earn your trust?
    When you make a decision, is it really yours?
    The next time you have a decision to make, take two sheets of paper. On one, write down all your personal experience on the issue. On the other, write down other people's opinions and all you have read or been told about the subject.
    Then throw away the second piece of paper.
    Look back at the first piece of paper.
    What is your decision, based on your experience?

2   What three things would you attempt if you thought you could not fail? Write them down on a sheet of paper.
    Why are you not attempting them now?
    Write the reasons on another sheet of paper.
    Now look at the second sheet of paper. How sure are you that these are real obstacles to achieving the things you want to do?

3   Listen for a day and count the number of times that you are about to confess out loud to being unable to do something or not very good at something. Stop yourself before you do so. How do you feel about that? Remember you do not have to say you *are* good at something, just don't say you can't do it or are bad at it.

4   Fill in the 'Beliefs in Time' worksheet for one topic that interests you. Now think about what your parents believed about the same thing. If you do not know, guess what they believed from what they did. How similar are your beliefs about this topic to those of your parents?

5   Take one of your important goals and put it through the 'Identifying Limiting Beliefs' worksheet. What beliefs might stop you achieving this goal?

CHAPTER 8

TRANSITION

Leaving England to live with Andrea in Brazil was a big change for me. England had been home for a long time. I knew I wanted to live in Brazil and be with Andrea, and so I had to deal with a new country, language and culture. I was adrift from the surroundings that I knew and that had made my life stable. At the beginning, I did not have the security of the familiar, nor did I feel completely secure about the new environment. Often I was frightened. There were times when I would look at the purple São Paulo sky and feel lost. My old habits did not work; I could not make myself easily understood. There were also all the practical issues of transporting my possessions to Brazil from England. I spent many hours on the telephone finding out about shipping costs, customs and excise charges. I was a reluctant learner in the world of international transportation. Moving to another country means more than an air ticket and a big suitcase. I wholeheartedly desired the change, but there was the transition to weather. I would not have moved except for Andrea, and she was the person who helped me, supported me and believed in me to make the transition possible.

Transition is the most difficult time in coaching. The client is no longer in their old situation, but has not yet moved completely to the new situation. They have lost the security of the old and not yet attained the benefits of the new. They are in limbo and this can be very uncomfortable. At this stage the client has to trust the coach and trust their own resources. The support will be there if they can change their way of thinking.

Transition is like the split-second when you step forward – you are neither where you came from nor where you are going. You have to make a leap of faith without knowing if you are going to have a happy landing. There is a moment in the film *Indiana Jones and the Last Crusade* that perfectly illustrates the transition point. Our intrepid hero, Indiana Jones, played by Harrison Ford, faces his final ordeal before he can enter the sanctuary of the Holy Grail, the greatest prize of his life. He needs it desperately to heal his father, who has been shot by the Nazis. They are also after the Grail for their own evil purposes. Indiana Jones steps to the edge of what looks like a bottomless chasm, yet he must pass over it. The other side is too far for him to jump and there is no bridge that he can see. He has to trust that it is possible to cross, although he does not know how. He steps out into space without knowing there is anything to support him – and we see that his foot has landed on a thin bridge built of stone. The bridge has been there all the time, only he did not see it because from his viewpoint (and ours) the coloured stone of the bridge blends so perfectly into the rocks behind it that it is invisible. We only see it as the camera pans round to a different angle and our hero, heaving a sigh of relief, has the support he needs to cross the chasm.

THE TRANSITION MODEL ⬇

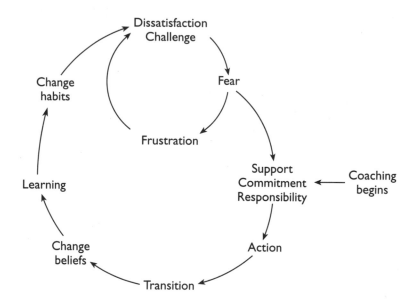

Transition model

Here is our model of transition showing the complete cycle of coaching. The client starts from the top with some form of dissatisfaction or challenge. They want a change. They want to be happier, although they may not yet be clear about where they want to be instead.

At the next stage, they have to deal with fear of change. This fear can keep them in their difficult situation – they can be frozen with fear and unable to react. This makes them frustrated and the frustration leads to further dissatisfaction. 'Slingshot coaching' is when the client circles around until the situation gets so bad or they get so frustrated that they propel themselves out of the ring like a slingshot. 'Slingshot coaching' is painful, but better than nothing.

Once out of the fear and frustration cycle, the client needs the support of the coach. The coaching relationship provides a structure to support the client and move them towards their goals. Once they take action, they reach the crucial point – the transition.

This transition model is about double loop coaching because limiting beliefs may be part of the obstructions that stop the client moving forward. Once past the transition point they will change their beliefs about themselves, other people and what is possible.

One issue that needs to be dealt with is loss. Loss can seem like a little death; the client needs to say goodbye to a part of themselves. I remember leaving England to be with Andrea in Brazil. Leaving the country I had lived in all my life was not an easy decision; it had many things I valued and still value – the colours of the trees in autumn, the chill in the September air, the taste of Cadbury's chocolate and Marmite, to name a few. Andrea helped me to change how I thought about this in a simple way. She proposed changing just one word. Instead of thinking about *losing* things, I started thinking about *leaving* things. Losing something is not a happy thought; it implies that it is something that is out of your control. *Leaving* something is a choice. When you leave something, you decide to leave it. When I thought about leaving England (and not losing things that I value), it was much easier to manage the transition. This was when Andrea first drew the transition model.

Once past the transition, a whole new world is there for the taking. This was certainly true when I began to live in Brazil: learning the language and speaking it (badly, at least to begin with), watching that purple sky of São Paulo turn darker in the twilight, eating new food in new places and paying with new currency, spending Christmas day on the beach in the sunshine, and loving every minute of it. I made wonderful new friends and we communicated in five languages – sign language, body language, music Portuguese and English. I also appreciated my friends in England in a new way – they were all wonderful in supporting me in making the change, and I really discovered what friendship meant.

There is so much to learn when you emerge on the other side of a transition. One thing you learn is to change your habits. Not only did it stop old habits (for example working alone and until the early hours of the morning), but you must also learn new ones (for example working with another person and sharing experiences).

Finally, having made the transition, there are a whole new set of challenges to deal with. So this transition model is really three-dimensional. Imagine it as a spiral coming off the page, moving upwards into dreams beyond the dream you are currently fulfilling.

HABITS

Habits are what we do when we don't think. They are very useful. We do not want to think about everything we do, we only want to think about the interesting things. The habits that work well for us are great. They give our life stability. However, when we want to change, our habits resist that change. To change your life, to get through the transition, you will need to change some habits and form new ones.

Once you want to change, habits can be a problem. You are a giant, you have tremendous strength, but lots of little habits can keep you tethered in place like the ropes that bound Gulliver in the book *Gulliver's Travels*. He woke up on the beach tied down by hundreds of very thin ropes tied by very small people (the Lilliputians). He was strong enough to break any single rope, but hundreds of them held him fast. He was helpless, and we may feel the same in the grips of our habits.

Many habits are formed early in life and we never really examine them. One of my friends told me how elephants are tamed in India. When they are young and not very strong, one foot is tethered to a stake in the ground. The young elephant tries to pull free but cannot, and gives up. As the elephant grows stronger, it stays tethered; it never tries again to break free, even though as a full-grown adult it could do so easily. It has obviously decided that the rope is too strong and given up trying.

What keeps habits in place? NLP uses the term *anchoring*. Anchoring is how a stimulus becomes a trigger that makes us respond in a certain way. An anchor is any visual, auditory or kinaesthetic trigger that is associated with a particular response or emotional state.

Anchors keep us in place, just as a ship's anchor stops it from drifting from its mooring. Our life stays steady because we surround ourselves with anchors that back up our way of being. Look around your room. What do you see? There could be a photograph of your family that makes you smile and feel good. That's an anchor for good feelings.

When you read the paper or watch television, advertisers are frantically trying to anchor good feelings to their product by showing people having fun, so that when you go to the supermarket, you won't just see a cleaner, you will associate it with having fun cleaning and will therefore want to buy it. Or when you see a particular supermarket, you will immediately think of low prices and good quality. Perhaps a little tune will pop into your head and you will be drawn to shop there.

Anchors can be visual, like people, clothes and cars. They can be auditory, like a particular piece of music, an advertising jingle or the voice of a dear friend. They can be kinaesthetic, like the feel of your favourite clothes, sitting in your armchair or the warmth of a hot bath. They can be olfactory or gustatory, like the smell of a hospital (why do they all smell the same?) or the taste of coffee or chocolate (Lindt!). Words can be anchors because they evoke ideas; your name is a powerful anchor for your identity. Anchors evoke emotional states and most of the time we do not notice the anchors, only the states. Some anchors are neutral. Some put us into good states. Others put us into bad states. From a coaching perspective, it does not matter if feelings that the anchor evokes are good or bad. What matters is that they are habitual.

The first step towards change is to be aware of what you have in the present moment. So one important part of coaching is to make the client aware of the everyday anchors in their lives. There is a worksheet for this (*see Resources, page 189*). Once a client is aware of the power of anchors, they will see how certain anchors trigger certain habits. If they want to change, they may need to change certain habits. This will mean:

1   being aware of the anchors that support the habit
2   creating a new habit to support the change
3   making new anchors to support the new habit

Here is one example. When I (Joseph) was living in London, I worked with a desktop computer. I was very used to this computer and had built up many habits that helped me work with it. I had my desk space organized around it; I knew where all my papers were. It was a great anchor for sitting down and doing good work – it was an anchor for a resourceful, concentrated state.

When I moved to Brazil, I had to leave this computer behind. I had to leave all my working habits behind, habits that I had painstakingly built up over the years into a regime that worked well. They were not bad habits, but all of them had to go and I had to build a whole new set of anchors around working with my laptop. The laptop was smaller and my working space in our new Brazilian office was different. After an initial period when I felt lost, I created a whole new set of anchors; now I feel even more creative. Not only can I work with my laptop in a different office, but I can also work with it anywhere in the world. It has become an even more powerful anchor for a concentrated working state, not just in the office, but also in a hotel room or even on an aeroplane. This took some effort, but it was completely supported by my new goals and values.

One empowering belief that helped me was that I was stronger than my habits. Habits were something I had built and therefore something I could dismantle. The future would be better than the past. I was sure of that. Changing these anchors was part of making my future the way I wanted it to be. Sitting, now, in that desired future, I am happy.

AWARENESS

When we respond to anchors we are not aware of the present moment. We go onto automatic pilot and lose ourselves for a time. Coaching is exploring the present and designing the future. Both need awareness of the present moment. A coach is an awakener to what is happening right now. Clients need to be aware of the present moment, otherwise they will not see how they are maintaining their problem. Their journey is a succession of 'nows', so they need to pay attention. 'Now' is the connection between the present and the future.

Habits are like little trances: we stop thinking. They are like rivers, they carry you along in a certain direction, but you are not aware you are moving until you resist the current. One of the great gifts a coach can give a client is the opportunity to step out of the current and to look at aspects of their life from a detached yet resourceful position. This is the intention of self-observation exercises. These exercises are in some ways spiritual practices, because they make you a witness of your life and you can reflect on what you are doing, rather than acting without thought. Once you have observed yourself in this way, you will be clearer about what changes you need to make.

We strongly suggest you give your clients some self-observation exercises. You can design them for each client, depending on their issues. With a self-observation exercise the intention is simply to be aware of what you are doing without feeling that you should change it or that it is bad. *Self-observation is not about changing anything*. There is no judgement, just observation. Change comes later.

Designing a Self-observation Exercise

1   Clarify the issue for a client. What do they want to explore? What are they dissatisfied with in their life?
2   Next, state the objective of the exercise in this form: 'I [client] want to become more aware of [the issue].'
3   Give the client a small number of questions to answer when they are alone and in a relaxed and resourceful state. They are to review their actions from a detached position, like watching a movie. They watch themselves, the star of the movie, but do not criticize or judge.

Here are two examples of self-observation exercises.

Client issue: Being caught up in too many habits, not being creative.
Objective of the exercise: To become more aware of habits.

Action Steps

1   Make a list of things that you repeat every day.
2   Each day for one week, select a habit from that list.
3   At the end of each day, find a time and a place where you can be alone
    and relaxed. Relax, breathe deeply, take the habit for the day and ask
    yourself the following questions:
    'What triggers this habit?'
    'How do I feel when I act because of this habit?'
    'How do other people react to me when I am acting because of this
    habit?'
4   Then record the answers in a journal for discussion at the next
    coaching session.

Client issue: Being uncomfortable when talking with their boss and
generally uncomfortable when dealing with people in authority.
Objective of the exercise: To become aware of current ways of dealing with
people with authority.

Action Steps

1   For the next week, pause twice a day, once at lunchtime and once at the
    end of the day. Find a place where you can be alone and relax for a few
    minutes. Relax and breathe deeply. Review the day so far and ask
    yourself these questions:
    'What reactions did I have to people in authority today?'
    'How did I feel at the time?'
    'What was I trying to achieve in those meetings?'
    'What was the reaction I got?'
    'What (if anything) stopped me from feeling comfortable?'
2   Write down the answers in a journal and review them at the next
    coaching session.

A journal is an important learning aid for the client for three reasons:

1   It encourages them to make notes of what they learn.
2   They have the material fresh in their mind to discuss with the coach.
3   They can review the journal every month and notice their progress. It is very easy for
    clients to forget how far they have come and what they have learned.

RELATIONSHIPS IN TRANSITION

Helping a client in their relationships is an important part of coaching. Relationships are part of the transition process and they can hinder it or help it. Other people confirm who we are by how they treat us, and if a client changes, then their relationships will change too, for the other people will not be able to treat them in the same way (although they may still try to).

Perceptual positions are a marvellous resource to help clients in every aspect of their relationships. When the client wants to clarify or explore their relationship with their partner, their children, their boss or a member of their work team, use the following process.

The Relationship-coaching Pattern

1   Ask the client to describe the relationship from first position – their point of view. Ask them to go back and imagine being with that other person in a typical situation. Get them to imagine that situation as vividly as possible: what was the room like, the colours, the time of day? Make sure they are really back in that situation.

2   Ask them to clarify what is going on for them in that relationship with the following questions:
'What are your goals in this situation?'
'What are you trying to achieve?'
'What is important to you in this situation?'
'What are you paying attention to?'
'What are you doing to achieve your goal?'
'How do you view the other person and how would you describe them (angry, whining, apologetic, dishonest, etc)?'
Is there a conflict at any level about beliefs and values, or skills, or behaviour?

3   Once you have drawn out this information, distract the client and get them to think about something else to 'break state'.

4   When they are ready, ask them to go to second position with the other person. If they protest that they do not want to, say that they do not have to sympathize or agree with the other person. This is only an exercise to try to understand their point of view in order to resolve any conflict in the best way. Many conflicts are because we do not understand our opponent.
Get the client to actually move to another chair and become the other

person as far as possible – they must assume the other person's physiology and way of speaking as far as they can. When they say 'I' in this position, they are talking as the other person. They will refer to their real self by their real name. Ask them the same questions and get them to answer as the other person:

'What are your goals in this situation?'

'What are you trying to achieve?'

'What is important to you in this situation?'

'What are you paying attention to?'

'What are you doing to achieve your goal?'

'How do you view the other person (that is yourself) and how would you describe yourself from this position (self-justifying, persecuting, nagging, incomprehensible, etc)?'

Understanding others comes from our shared humanity. Even if the other person is very different, this exercise will yield valuable insights for the client. It can be very interesting to draw out as much as possible about how that person sees the world; this is very helpful to the client.

If the client slips back into first position and starts to refer to themselves as 'I', remind them that they should be in second position. They will discover things about the other person that they could never have got in first position.

5   Break state and bring them back to themselves.

6   Now ask the client to stand halfway between first and second position where they can see both. From this third position, get them to coach themselves in first position.

What do they see in this relationship?

What do those two people agree about?

Where is the conflict?

What advice would you give yourself in first position?

7   Break state.

8   Now take the client back to first position and sit them down in their original chair. What advice will they take from themselves in third position?

How has this clarified the relationship and what have they learned?

What will they do differently the next time they meet this other person?

Give the client a specific task to do next time they meet the other person to test their insights from this exercise.

9   Finally, what was the client's experience of taking the three positions? Which of the three positions was easiest for them to adopt?

> If they have a preference for one position, a further task could be for
> them to make a list of the drawbacks of that position. (For example, if
> you have a strong first position, you might be considered opinionated.
> A strong second position can lead you into neglecting your own
> interests.) Finally, ask them to make a list of the benefits that they
> would get from developing the other two positions.

This exercise will help the client in that relationship and a fluency in each position and knowledge of their preferred one will help them in every relationship from now on.

To illustrate this technique, here is one example of a coaching session we supervised. James was the coach, Michael the client. Michael wanted to work on his relationship with his 12-year-old daughter Audrey, who was learning the piano.

Michael was nagging Audrey to practise the piano in the morning before she went to school, but he did not like doing this; he wanted her to enjoy playing for herself. Audrey of course was finding devilishly creative ways to avoid the practice – suddenly there were more important things to do in the morning and the piano practice time was squeezed out. This annoyed Michael, because Audrey had promised to practise.

Furthermore, Michael and his wife had previously agreed that *she* would make sure Audrey practised. Michael felt his wife was not fulfilling her part of the bargain and solved the problem by taking on the responsibility himself while resenting having to do so.

Michael did not begrudge Audrey the money for her piano lessons, but he wanted her to get the most from them. He himself had learned the piano when he was young with a very bad teacher. He had given up, but now wished he had continued. (Here is a great temptation for a coach to do some therapy to explore why and how Michael might be nagging his daughter to live out something that he himself wanted and regretted he had not done in his own childhood. James resisted this temptation.) Michael could still play a little and liked to play simple duets with Audrey. Audrey enjoyed this too.

After listening to this story, James asked Michael a powerful question: 'What would be a great outcome for you?'

Notice this follows the *what ... you ... verb ... future positive* model of questions.

Michael replied he wanted the practice to be a fun time. He did not want to be a nagging parent, but a fun parent. He wanted the piano to be enjoyable for Audrey. The value of fun also came in strongly here – and it was definitely lacking in the situation as Michael had described it.

'What's below wanting to be a good parent; what's important?' Here James was digging a little deeper into the values behind the goal.

Michael replied that he wanted Audrey to enjoy learning and said with particular emphasis that he wanted a *great* long-term relationship with her.

James said that clearly both Michael and Audrey had a positive intention, even though they were quarrelling about how to achieve this. Then he asked, 'What do you do to get her to practise?'

Michael said he had 'tried' a lot of things. He would help Audrey when she was practising and play duets with her.

James said that this is what he did once she was *already practising*, but what did he do to make her practise?

'I nag,' said Michael.

Michael described how he would get upset with Audrey for not practising, with his wife for not doing her duty in dealing with Audrey's practice and with himself for getting annoyed.

What Michael was paying attention to was his *own* feelings of frustration and his *own* need to get Audrey to practise.

James then took Michael to second position. He invited him to become Audrey and sit in the chair opposite. He helped him enormously by putting him into the specific situation in the morning in his house: what he was seeing as Audrey, what he was hearing as Audrey and what he was feeling as Audrey.

As Audrey, Michael said several things:

'I hate being told what to do.'
'Why doesn't Dad leave me alone?'
'Why is he always so busy in the morning?'
'I want him to come and play the piano with me.'

James then did a little coaching on Michael (as Audrey), asking her what she wanted and what was important to her. He found out that she liked her piano teacher and it was important to her to play the piano because many of her friends played.

Next James took Michael to a third position, standing away from the two chairs and equidistant between them.

'What do you think of what is happening between them?' he asked.

Michael in third position could see that Audrey wanted to practise, but did not want to be nagged. Nagging was taking away her pleasure in playing the piano. In third position he was able to coach himself in first position. He saw that he should clarify with his wife who was going to help Audrey with her playing. He also thought the word 'practice' was turning into a negative word for her. Instead, he would invite her to 'play' duets with him in the morning. When they had done that and were both enjoying it, she would have the momentum to continue for the rest of the time that morning. The more he could make it fun for her, the more it would be fun for him and the more she would value the playing.

He went back to his first-position chair.

James asked him, 'What will you do next?' This was an invitation to a task.

Michael replied he would speak to his wife and clarify who would take responsibility for reminding Audrey to practise in the morning. Also, for the next week, he would play duets with Audrey on each of her practice days and see the difference it made to both of them.

A week later Michael reported back a complete success. He had improved his relationship with his daughter. This was much better feedback than getting his daughter to practise, even though that was his first stated goal. The coaching had reached to the value behind the goal – the good relationship – and Michael was getting more of that. Audrey was also practising more.

In this example, James did not take Michael to fourth position. Fourth position is the position of the system, in this case Michael's family. However, he could see, even in third position, that there was an effect on the family and this covered two important areas: his relationship with his daughter and his relationship with his wife.

In relationship coaching like this, you can also use the wheel of perspectives. You can use the four spaces for the four perceptual positions or you can use different perspectives, depending on the context you are exploring with your client. For example in business coaching, you might explore a work situation from the point of view of a manager, a customer, the CEO and the business brand. Ask the client to take each of these perspectives to get insights into the situation. Write the insights into the spaces provided.

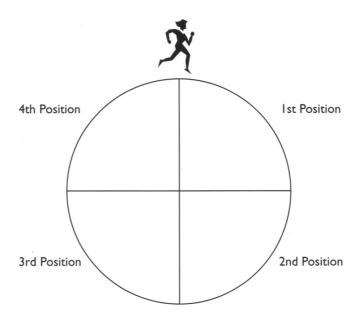

The wheel of perspectives

TASKING

Many clients have a good intellectual knowledge of their situation, but nothing changes. They are on the level of *knowing*, but this level alone is not enough to make a change.

The next stage is *wanting*. Clients want to change, but this is not enough either. They need to know *how* to make a change. A coach can make a big difference here by helping the client free themselves from the habits and beliefs that are holding them back and helping them find the best strategies for change.

This leads to the last step: doing. This completes the cycle. Without this step everything that comes before remains as potential only and will not make a difference. Hence the emphasis coaching puts on the client doing something different.

What distinguishes coaching from most other approaches is this emphasis on action learning. The coach is constantly asking the client to do something different, to challenge their habits, to become more self-aware, to challenge their beliefs or live their values, and this is embodied in a task.

A task is something the coach asks the client to do as a result of their progress in the session. Tasks are always precise and specific. They need to be clear in four areas:

1 'What will you do?' (the task itself)
2 'When will you do it?' (the time scale)
3 'Who is involved?' (the other people)
4 'When will we discuss what happened?' (The coach needs feedback about what happened.)

Tasks are always action-oriented – they involve doing something. The cognitive understanding comes afterwards. In that sense tasks represent a leap of faith. This is why rapport is particularly important. Tasks are not always comfortable for the client and a client will not accept a task unless it is framed as a learning experience, *not* as an assignment which they must succeed in doing.

The most important characteristic of a task is that the client learns something about their own resources, regardless of whether they 'succeed' or 'fail'.

The learning is in the feedback, not a successful result.

Tasks can be framed in two ways: as a challenge and as a request.

A Challenge

A challenge stretches the client beyond their self-imposed limits. When you challenge a client with a task, you demonstrate that you believe in them and their potential to do more than they are doing. Make the challenge realistic and not impossible, but stretch the client sufficiently for them to test their belief about themselves. When you do this you act as the client's champion, you stand up for them, you demonstrate that you believe in them, even if they themselves do not.

A client may meet your challenge with frank incredulity, in which case you may need to tone it down or negotiate another challenge. Yet even if the client does not complete the challenge, they will learn a lot from attempting it and their achievement will still be greater than they thought.

No one achieves the impossible unless they attempt the seemingly impossible.

A Request

A request is simpler than a challenge and more achievable. It is asking a client to further their goals by taking a specific action. A request will not stretch the client like a challenge, but often they will be reluctant to carry it out.

A request should be precise. The client should know exactly what to do to carry it out and what the result will be.

It is usually best to preface any request or challenge by saying 'I have a request…' The client will then give you permission to go ahead and will be more receptive because they have been warned that they are about to be asked something.

It is very important that all requests have a deadline, for example, 'I have a request for you. Will you talk to your son about his problem before our next meeting in a week's time?'

Teaching clients how to make clear requests themselves can be extremely powerful in a coaching relationship. Many clients are unable to be assertive or feel resentful when people ask them to do things. They may also feel guilty when they say 'no'. Yet they may feel they are not getting what they want out of life because they do not make clear requests of the people around them. When the coach provides a model of how to make clear requests, they help the client to ask for what they want as well.

Simple and Complex Tasks

Requests and challenges can be quite simple, for example:

Read a book.
See a movie.
Watch a video.
Go dancing.
Learn to sing, or sing in public.
Talk to children.
Tell stories to children.
Talk in front of mirror.

Join an amateur dramatic society and act in a play.
Wear different clothes.
Change the wrist on which you wear your watch.
Buy a different newspaper from your usual one.
Change your home furniture around.

Tasking may involve more complex actions:

↓ *Create an ordeal.* If, for example, the client is afraid of their boss and unable to deal with people in positions of authority, you can task them to get an experience of resources in another context that they can use. You might ask them to go rock climbing. If they accept, they can generalize this courage to other parts of their life. After all, if they can go rock climbing, asking their boss for a rise can't be so hard, can it?

↓ *Prescribe the symptom.* It then comes under their control, because they are doing it deliberately. For example, if someone suffers badly from nerves and shakes before and during a speech, ask them to publicly state that at the beginning of the speech to everyone and to 'try' to feel more nervous. They will find that acknowledgement makes the nerves much weaker. Problems like anxiety and nervousness derive much of their power from the resistance we have to them.

↓ *Model another person.* You can ask the person to model another person who has the resources they themselves need to answer the question or solve the problem.

Responses

The client has three possible responses to a request or a challenge:

↓ *'Yes.'* The client agrees. They then become accountable for the task.

↓ *'No.'* The client refuses. They do not agree with the task or you do not have the rapport to make it at that time. Maybe they are not yet ready to carry it out.

↓ *Negotiation.* The client is open to the task but wants to negotiate the details or has a counterproposal that they feel more comfortable about and that they believe would forward the action in the same way.

Beware when a client says they will 'try' to carry out a task. It usually means they will not, or they assume it is difficult. The word 'try' implies difficulty, even impossibility. If they say they will 'try', ask them to commit to 'yes', 'no' or 'it depends'. Then you can negotiate a different task if necessary. Also beware when a client says, 'I could do that.' Ask them to say, 'I will do that!'

Results

When you give a task, the client may do it and learn something important. This is the best result, but it does not always turn out this way. A client may forget to do a task. If the client has taken responsibility for the task, then this is significant. How did they forget? You may need to check their commitment and support them by setting an anchor to remind them. You will talk about the result at the next session. If a client forgets a task or does not find time to do it for two sessions in a row, then they are not congruent about that task, whatever they say, and you need to discuss this fully. Never blame the client. It is their task, their responsibility and their life. There is always something to learn, even from forgetfulness.

Another possibility is that the client does the task, but does not think they got a good result. The coach and client can talk about this. What did the client expect? What have they learned from the result? You might need to give them another task with the same intention.

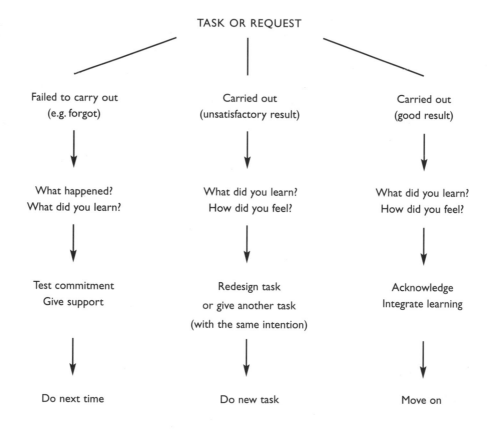

Tasking possibilities

Accountability

Throughout the coaching process, the client owns the results and is accountable for the *results*. Coach and client together are responsible for the *process*. They are in partnership. The fact that the client owns the result does not mean that the coach has no responsibility for giving their best in the process. Client and coach work together in a partnership where one and one make more than two if they work with synergy. The relationship is the same as in sports coaching. Remember that when an athlete wins a trophy, they are the one who stands on the winner's podium, cheered by the crowd. The coach does not join them on the podium, even though they worked together to achieve that result. The athlete may acknowledge the part played by the coach, but it is the athlete who gets the result and the glory.

This means that the client must take responsibility. They take responsibility for their actions and therefore their life.

Responsibility can sound a heavy burden. For many people it is anchored to being blamed if something goes wrong. But in coaching terms it is spelled 'response-ability': the ability to respond. Clients are able to respond to the tasks, requests and challenges that the coach sets.

There are three basic questions for the client to make them accountable for their actions or tasks:

1 'What are you going to do?'
  What actions is the client going to take? These should be specific, timed actions based on the client's goals and values. They may be tasks, requests or challenges from the coach, or the client themselves may decide what to do, based on the coaching session. Notice the question follows the *what ... you ... verb ... future positive* pattern.

2 'When will you do it?'
  All actions must have a schedule or they are likely to be empty promises. Negotiate a deadline that is clear and realistic. Many times people think that it would be a 'good idea' if they did something, but as often as not it remains in the realm of a good idea and is never translated into action. This question makes sure that it is.

3 'How will you know?'
  The action will have definite results. The coach needs to know the action has been taken. The client may telephone after they have finished it, or fax or e-mail the coach. They may leave the discussion until the next coaching session.

Before, during and after the transition, the client needs support. The coach can support them in two ways – by helping them to mentally rehearse what they want to do and by helping them to set supportive anchors in their life.

Mental Rehearsal

What happens in the outside world must first happen in the inner world, so teach your clients to mentally rehearse their goals and tasks. This will make them real in their mind so that later they will manifest in the outside world.

Mental rehearsal works. But like any process, you need to follow certain rules. You can teach this next pattern to your clients during one of the first coaching sessions so they can use it themselves whenever they want.

Mental Rehearsal Process

1   Set the goal. See it in detail so you are absolutely clear about what you will have to do to achieve it.

2   Relax. See yourself *doing* the task exactly as you want. It is important that you *see yourself* in a dissociated mental picture. You should not yet imagine yourself actually doing it. You should be like a director of your own movie where you are the star.

3   Make this movie as perfect as possible. Imagine as much detail as you can – where you are, the clothes you are wearing, who is there with you. Use all your representational systems. See the pictures as clearly as you can. Hear the sounds, feel your body movements, including your sense of balance. The richer the detail, the more powerful the process.

4   Once you are satisfied, you should associate into the picture, that is, imagine doing it for real. See what you would see if you were doing it. Hear what you would hear. Notice the other people in the scene and how they are reacting.

5   If it does not feel right, go back and see yourself in the movie again and make further adjustments.

6   When you are completely happy with what you see, store it as a private videotape in your personal Blockbuster collection. You can see it at any time you like.

Structures

Structures are the anchors that the coach helps the client create to remind the client of their vision, goals or values or actions that need to be taken.

For example, one client took a picture that was hanging in his home office and turned it upside down. Whenever he saw that (and he came into the office every working day), it reminded him that there were other, more creative ways of looking at any situation. This was a structure that he set up to help him take new perspectives and be more creative. Another client put his wristwatch on the other arm to help him remember to set the alarm clock so that he would get up earlier in the morning to meditate. Clients have good intentions but sometimes they need help to remember, because habits may make it likely that they will forget. The coach allies themselves with the client's best self – the self that wants to change to be more and have a fuller life.

Structures, like anchors, can be visual, auditory or kinaesthetic. Be creative when you set up structures for your clients.

Examples of structures are:

marking calendars
leaving yourself voicemail messages
setting your watch or mobile telephone to give an alarm at a certain time
putting post-it notes with affirmations around the house
listening to a relaxation tape
finding an exercise partner
choosing a new piece of music to listen to on the Walkman
putting a photograph on your desk

We get used to structures, however, and they are not likely to work so well after a certain time (usually one to two months). After that, you will need to brainstorm new structures with the client.

You can help a client build structures by asking questions like:

'What can you do that would help you remember this?'
'How can we track your progress with the task?'
'How will you remember to do this?'
'What can you do that will remind you to take this action regularly?'

COMPLETION

Finally there will come a point when the coach and the client decide that the work is finished. Of course, the work of achieving goals and living the associated values is never finished. The end of the coaching relationship is just punctuation in that process. Like a good teacher, the coach's work is done when they are no longer needed.

The criteria for the end of the coaching relationship should be decided at the beginning. The relationship will end when the coach and client agree that the client has achieved what they came to coaching to achieve, unless something dramatic occurs to stop the coaching.

At the end, the coach and client should see:

↓   Long-term sustained excellent performance in the client's chosen field. This will be measured by the standards of coach and client and also objective standards, independent of either.

↓   Self-generation and creativity. The client will be able to find their own ways to progress. They will become more self-reliant.

It is a wonderful feeling for both coach and client to finish a successful coaching relationship. The final session can be a debriefing of the coaching. You can ask the client:

'What worked best for you in this coaching relationship?'
'What did not work well for you?'
'What do you feel most proud of?'
'When were you most afraid?'
'When were you most surprised?'
'When did you feel most empowered?'
'What has changed most about you?'
'What has changed in your relationship with others?'
'What are your expectations about yourself now?'

SUMMARY

Transition
The transition model spans the full cycle of coaching.
The client begins with a problem or situation they want to change.
They have to deal with the fear of change and may become frustrated at lack of progress.

Once out of the fear and frustration cycle, they are in transition. They still need the support of the coach. The client takes responsibility and makes a commitment to change. The coaching relationship provides a structure to support the client and move them towards their goals.

Transition is the most delicate time in coaching. The client is no longer in their old situation, but has not yet moved completely to the new situation.

It is helpful if the client thinks of leaving things behind rather than losing things.

Habits

Habits give our life stability.

When we want to change, our habits resist that change.

To change your life, you will need to change some habits and form new ones.

Habits are kept in place by anchors.

An anchor is any visual, auditory or kinaesthetic trigger that is associated with a particular response or emotional state.

Most of the time we do not notice the anchors, only the states.

Some anchors are neutral. Some anchors put us into good states. Others may put us into bad states.

With the help of the coach, clients will:

   Become aware of the anchors that support their habits.

   Create new habits that support the change they want to make.

   Make new anchors to support the new habits.

The client needs to be aware of the present moment in order to explore the present and design the future.

A self-observation exercise is one powerful way for the client to appreciate where they are and how their habits are holding them in place.

Self-observation is not about changing anything, just observing without judgement.

It is very helpful if the client keeps a journal of their progress in the coaching.

Use first, second and third positions to help a client deal with their relationships.

Requests, Challenges and Tasks

Coaches get clients to take action by giving them tasks, challenges and requests.

A challenge stretches the client beyond their self-imposed limits.

A request asks the client to further their goals by taking a specific action.

A task is more complex than a request or a challenge.

The learning for the client is in the feedback, not in a successful result.

A client is accountable when they take responsibility for their actions and therefore their life.

There are three basic questions for the client to make them accountable for their actions or tasks:

'What are you going to do?'
'When will you do it?'
'How will you know?'

The client needs support from the coach. The coach can provide this in two ways:
teaching the client to mentally rehearse their goals
helping the client set anchors in their life

The coaching will end when the coach and client agree that the client has achieved what they came to coaching to achieve, unless something dramatic occurs to stop the coaching.

ACTION STEPS

If you want to understand, act. Here are some ways for you to explore the ideas in this chapter. You can also use them as tasks for your client and yourself if you wish.

1 Think of a change that took place in your life. Do you remember a transition point? What could have made the transition easier for you? Which habits did you change?

2 Take one habit that you have that you would like to change, for example biting your nails.
     What are the benefits of that habit?
     When did it start?
     How do you feel about it?
     How does it fit into your life now?
   Every time you are aware of it, stop for a moment and say, 'I choose to do this.' Notice how this changes your experience of the habit.

3 Start to develop your intuition about people. Be interested and watch people in restaurants and public places. Notice how they move. Notice how they are dressed. Guess their annual salary and their occupation. Guess their age. Now make up a short story about their life – where they were born and what sort of life they have had.
   This is fun to do and will sharpen your powers of observation.

4 **Develop a self-observation exercise for yourself with the objective of becoming more aware of your thoughts and judgements about your goals. Stop and relax at the end of each day.**
Sit down and relax.
Ask yourself the following questions and record the answers in your journal:
    'What is occupying my thoughts right now?'
    'Whom do I feel close to right now?'
    'Whom do I feel distant from right now?'
    'What goals have I worked on today?'
    'What will I do differently tomorrow?'

5 **Complete the Everyday Anchors worksheet (*page 194*).**
What does this tell you about your normal life and habits?
How can you increase the number of anchors in your life that put you in a good state?
How can you eliminate the number of anchors in your life that put you in a bad state?

6 **Pick one important relationship and use the wheel of perspectives (*page 195*).**
What do you think about this relationship from first position? Write your thoughts down in the first-position space.
Go to second position. Be the other person. What do you think about the relationship (as them)? Record your insights in the second-position space.
Review what you have written in the first and second-position spaces. How is this relationship? Record your thoughts in the third-position space.
What system are you both part of? How does the relationship fit into that system? How does the fact of being inside that system affect the relationship for good or ill?
Finally, what action will you take as a result of your insights?

⇨ THE DREAM CONTINUES...

⇨ ⇨ ⇨ Suddenly we are inside the cathedral and it is even bigger than we thought. The walls are very thick and are made by big pieces of dark stone that are very cold and wet to the touch.

Nobody outside could hear us shout for help in here. Every word we say seems to echo everywhere. The cathedral is listening to us and repeating what we say in its cold stony voice.

We hear the wind whistling through the alcoves.

Looking up, we see some stained-glass windows that give the place a soft light, but not enough to allow us to move around in safety. There are too many hard corners and uneven stones. We stay still and silent.

The woman appears at the front door, the light of the lamp making very long shadows on the floor and walls. She walks round with ease and lights some candles that make it much easier for us to see where we are and to decide where to go.

We see things now that were in darkness before, though some things still stay in darkness and we are glad of that.

The woman smiles.

We walk around exploring.

In one corner we find some beautiful pieces of art, forgotten for many years, the dust lying thickly and silently over them.

The woman is now struggling to open a small door that we didn't see before. She opens it with a loud noise that tells us that it has not been opened for years.

The light coming through the door is blinding for a moment in the semi-darkness that we have become used to.

We see a road of light leading to a metal spiral staircase.

We run there and stop short when we see some signs: 'STOP! DANGER! DO NOT PROCEED!'

We look back but the woman has disappeared... Why does she

disappear when we need her the most? She *must* tell us what to do!

These stairs seem to lead to the top of the building... We peer upwards, but cannot see beyond the first spiral.

What can be so dangerous about stairs?

Who wrote the signs?

PART 3

COACHING IN PRACTICE

CHAPTER 9

COACHING IN ACTION

⇨ ⇨ ⇨ We have given many tools and ideas about coaching in this book. Now it is time to put them together in a coaching session. How do we use all these ideas in practice?

Here is a coaching session that we conducted with a client who was having trouble deciding what sort of work to do. He had been a therapist for some years and one of his goals was to do some business coaching. His name was Robin.

Many transcripts only give the words of client and coach. However we believe that there is just as much information in the client's body language as the words, so we have described this where we think it is important.

Robin starts the session sitting on his hands with his legs crossed. This could be interpreted as being closed, but as we have not yet calibrated what this means to him, we are keeping an open mind.

Coach:　　　　　'What goal are you working on at the moment?'

Robin:　　　　　'I want to change my career direction. I have worked as a therapist for some years. I work mostly with people with problems – many are from the underprivileged parts of society – but I've always been interested in business. I still work as a therapist, but there is a duality in me.'

At this stage the coach is mirroring Robin's body language, sitting with his legs crossed and leaning forward.

Robin:　　　　　'Whether I do most of my work with those people as a therapist [*here he gestures to his left with both hands*] or in a business environment [*he gestures to his right*], it's partly about money. I can make more in a business environment and I want more money.'

At this stage, the coach already has a lot of information. There is a duality. On one hand (literally), Robin wants to continue to work as a therapist. On the other hand, he wants to work in the business environment, which would bring him more money. It is also interesting that the usual eye movement for a right-handed person (as Robin is) when visualizing is up to the left for remembered experiences and up to the right for constructed experiences. Remembered pictures usually come fromn the past, constructed ones could come from the future. From this, it is possible that in the way that Robin is thinking about it, working in therapy belongs to his past and the business environment belongs to his future. Robin is also saying that money is part of that decision. Money in itself is not a value, but it can buy many things that Robin would value. The coach needs to know the values behind both parts. Only then can Robin make a decision or come to a compromise.

Next, the coach backtracks.

Coach:	'So on one hand [*gestures to Robin's right*] you want to work in the business environment. On the other hand [*gestures to Robin's left*] you still value your work as a therapist with people who have problems. You say that money is important in this.'
Robin nods.	
Coach:	'So this is what the situation looks like on the outside [*gestures to right and left and again anchors the two different situations, one to each side*]… How does this relate to different aspects of yourself?'
Robin pauses for thought.	
Robin:	'The left is familiar, comfortable and appeals to my value of helping people. So many people have problems that they do not deserve. I hate it when children are involved too.'
Coach:	'Helping people?' [*Backtracking the value.*]
Robin, nodding:	'The other hand appeals to my need for recognition and freedom.'
Coach:	'OK, so we have a shorthand way of describing different parts of yourself… The therapy part is about helping people?'
Robin nods.	
Coach:	'And the business part is about recognition and freedom.'
Robin nods again.	

At this stage the coach has rapport and has firmly anchored the two aspects, business on the right and therapy on the left. The first level of values of each is clear: recognition/helping people. The goal is somehow to harmonize the two parts, but how is not yet clear.

Coach:	'Could we imagine what they would look like in terms of what we would see, or what would be typical of you when you are working in the two different environments?'

Robin, looking down and in a low soft voice:

> 'I have a picture and a very clear feeling about the therapy part of myself. It is very comfortable, very much in its own feelings and very low key.'

At this stage, the coach deliberately starts to gesture a little differently, making more circular gestures so the two sides are not so clearly marked.

The coach asks the next question softly and slowly to match the client's voice tone.

Coach:	'We have a picture [*Robin has said so*] and we have a voice tone [*low key*] that's over there [*gestures to the left*]… Anything else?'
Robin:	'Yes. [*Laughs.*] I am wearing really old clothes!'
Coach:	'OK. Now what about the other?'

Robin gestures and laughs, suddenly very animated.

Robin:	'This is really great! It's smart, it looks really good, I see myself going into a business and sitting down at the boardroom. I am wearing completely different clothes. Very nice suits.'

At this stage the coach notices that the therapy part is represented mainly through the auditory and kinaesthetic representational systems, the business part predominantly through the visual system.

Coach, animated, speaking much more quickly to match Robin's voice tone:

> 'You have very clear ideas of what these two Robins look like and they appear pretty separate at the moment.'

The coach is acknowledging the visual aspect of the business side by saying they *appear* separate.

Robin, speaking fast:

> 'I can get out and just go for it regardless… [*pauses and slows down*], but then the therapy side says, "What you are doing is not worthwhile. It doesn't make a difference to real people's lives, it's all a bit bloodless."'

This 'Yes, but…' is sequentially incongruent. The values are different, the representational systems are different and the voice tones are different – one after the other.

Robin:	'They are now out here!' [*Gestures expansively even further to his left and right.*]
Coach:	'So we have made them further apart by clarifying them.' [*Makes big gestures.*]

Robin: 'Yes.'

Coach: 'And the therapy part thinks it is not worthwhile. Worthwhile …
                  what does that get for you?'

The coach is looking for the values behind the goal.

Robin, looking down to the right, and answering in a low tone:

                  'Everything. It's wonderful. It's a privilege. I really make a
                  difference.'

Coach: 'And making a difference, what does that get for you? [*Still asking
                  if there are any more core values.*] What is important about making
                  a difference?'

Robin, looking down to the right:

                  'Feeling my heart. I can really go for that. I feel everything is
                  worthwhile, that I have affected people in a deep way and it is
                  really rewarding. I feel privileged. There is a feeling of needing to
                  be needed. I don't really want to go into that…'

Coach: 'That may be one aspect of it, but it is not necessary to go into it at
                  all. [*Resisting the invitation to do therapy.*] Clearly there is a lot of
                  feeling here. And there is a feeling about privilege…' [*The coach
                  marks out the word in the same way as Robin did with his voice
                  tone.*]

It is interesting too, that Robin started by saying he works with underprivileged people
and this *gives* him privilege.

Robin: 'Yes, privilege.'

Coach, backtracking:

                  'Privilege, helping people, making a difference…'

Robin: 'Hmm…' [*Agrees but stays looking down, lost in thought.*]

Coach: 'We have some strong values and emotions behind this work and
                  we must take those into account.'

Robin: 'Yes.'

The coach has calibrated Robin's voice tone, which is different again from before. These
values seem to be the core values in his goal of working with underprivileged people.

Coach, shifting voice tone and speaking more quickly:

                  'In terms of the business part over here [*gestures*], what is
                  important about that?'

The coach is now going to find out the core values behind the business part.

Robin: 'I think it is about external validation and confirmation that what I do is worthwhile.'

Coach: 'And that external confirmation, what is important about that?'

Robin closes his eyes and furrows his brow as if trying to see something with difficulty on his mental screen.

Robin: 'I have had a lot of training, so that investment would be worthwhile. Other people would tell me that it had been worth it. [*He clenches his hands at the front of his body.*] Somehow that isn't over there and I don't know why. [*Noticing that his gestures are at the front.*] I want to know that investment of time and money is worth it.'

Coach: 'And if that investment in time and money is worth it, what is important about that? What is that worth?'

The coach is still digging for core values.

Robin: 'I don't know… Recognition… It needs to be recognized.' [*He crosses his hands on his lap.*]

Coach: 'So now I want to link that back to the other side. Correct me if I am wrong, but here there seems to be some sort of recognition in yourself. The therapy Robin does not care here about what other people think.'

Robin: 'No. Here, where I do therapy, recognizing myself is enough, no one else needs to do so.' [*Robin looks down and breathes deeply.*]

Coach: 'It feels as though [*using the representational system that Robin is using to think*] there is some kind of recognition here in both parts, but coming from different directions [*gestures to right and left*].'

Robin, smiling: 'Yes.'

This is a key point in this coaching session. The two different aspects have something in common: recognition. This is a key value for both.

Coach: 'So both parts want recognition for different aspects?'

Robin sits upright in a balanced position, but leaning slightly to the right.

Robin: 'I guess so.'

Coach: 'How could they work together, both getting the recognition that they want?'

This is the key question. Both parts need the value respected. Now we are coming to the second part of the coaching session – how to respect both parts, so Robin can use both. Robin looks into the distance, clearly visualizing.

Coach: 'How can "therapy Robin" help "business Robin" to get the external recognition he wants?'

Here the coach is asking the therapy Robin to help the business Robin to get something that is very important to the therapy Robin (recognition). How can he refuse?

Robin, blinking rapidly:

'On a practical level that is already happening. Hmm ... but inside me that is not happening. Inside I am completely split one or the other. I like the smart business part. I really have a need for people to see me out there in the business world. I want to be recognized. I want money. But I can't act like that over here [*points left*], and I can't act smart and businesslike over there [*points right*].'

Coach: 'Who is the real Robin?'

Robin: 'Maybe he is neither.'

Coach: 'Maybe he is the one who gets the recognition... How could you get your own internal recognition about helping people when you work in business?'

This question is designed to make Robin think about recognition in two different ways: recognition from himself and recognition from others.

Robin, looking down to his right and closing his eyes:

'Only by some kind of measurement.'

Coach: 'There is internal recognition – recognition by yourself. And there is external recognition – recognition by other people.'

The coach is working with the value of recognition.

Coach: 'It is important to you to make a difference and help people.'

The coach is acknowledging the Robin who wants to do therapy.

Robin: 'Yes.'

Coach: 'Don't you help people on the business side? How else could they recognize you?'

Robin: 'This sounds strange, even to me... Business somehow does not seem to be about real people, it's all at a distance...' [*Looks pensive and puzzled.*]

Coach: 'Businesses pay people money. Business helps people live. The clothes and the things made by business are for people. Business donates money to charity. How is business not about people?'

The coach is challenging Robin's unexamined belief that business is not about people.

Robin: 'Yes, it's ridiculous.'

Coach: 'So how do you imagine those two coming together?'

The coach is using very open language here, deliberately not saying exactly what 'those two' are. They could be the two types of recognition, they could be the two aspects of Robin or they could be the recognition and the business Robin.

Coach: 'You help people in the business environment matching that environment and you help people in the other environment matching that too. You get recognition from both...'

Robin, stroking his chin and looking up with his eyes closed: 'Mmmm...'

Coach: 'Imagine...'

Robin closes his eyes again.

Coach: 'Sorry, you are still thinking...'

Robin: 'I am just actually visualizing the two coming together at a central point.'

Coach, utilizing the idea of central:
'That is central to you, you put it there. What is central about the business part of you getting recognition and helping people?'

Robin is thinking with his hands together in front of his face.

Robin: 'The recognition that I get here [*gestures right, the business side*], will be the same thing that I do there [*gestures left, the therapy side*]. The work that I do right across the spectrum.' [*Makes an expansive gesture from left to right.*]

Coach: 'So the distinction between the business environment and other is big, yet the *work* that you do ... is the same for you and you will get recognition from yourself and from others for doing that work. And you do work that is good and makes a difference... And how does that feel – the work being central to you and getting recognition?'

The coach is bringing together the values common to both.

Robin is making balanced gestures at last – he is sitting upright with his hands
together in centre of his body.

Robin: 'It's far more clear and central…' [*Makes a circular gesture in the
middle of his body.*]

Coach: 'Tell me more about that.' [*Makes the same gesture.*]

Robin: 'Whirlwind … it's like a whirlwind. There is a lot of noise and
action at the edges, but it is still in the middle…' [*Laughs.*]

Coach: 'You are the same person and you can work across the spectrum
and you work and make a difference. You will be recognized
sometimes more by yourself and sometimes more by other
people. You can recognize yourself on the inside however they
recognize you on the outside. Can you see yourself doing that?
How does that feel?'

Robin, nodding and looking into the distance:

'Rather than try to put things together [*more circular gestures in
the middle*], I can move between them as long as I focus on my
work helping people. I feel comfortable.'

Coach: 'What does the therapy Robin have to say about that? How do you
feel about that?'

The coach is checking that the solution is acceptable to the therapy part using the auditory and kinaesthetic systems, as those are the ones he uses to talk about therapy.

Robin, laughing: 'I am going to get some new clothes! Now I will be able to afford
them!'

Coach: 'And how does the business Robin see the change?'

Robin: 'Good. I still have good feelings from there… [*Laughs and smiles.*]
I get a sense of more freedom of movement.'

Coach: 'Anything else about that?'

Robin: 'The business side of me has been given permission and feels
released. Up to now, I've been held back.'

The session ended with the coach giving Robin three tasks. One was to rethink his fee
structure for working, which had been too low, another was to buy some new clothes
and the third was to talk to a friend of his who is a senior manager in a business to get
further insights into how that business operates.

This session was essentially about making a decision. It was an impossible decision at
the start because it seemed as if there were two parts of Robin fighting and espousing
different values. What the coach did by listening, gaining rapport, matching language
and discovering values was to find the key value that brought the two aspects together,

so that both could feel fulfilled. Robin had two goals and they seemed to be irreconcilable. The key values were making a difference on both sides and recognition from Robin himself and from the outside world. It was the values that brought them together.

This is a little more complicated than many sessions where there is one goal and its associated values. The most difficult decisions are when goals seem incompatible and the values clash. It is essential to find the deeper values in order to find a good solution.

CHAPTER 10

COACHING YOURSELF

⇨ ⇨ ⇨ Much of this book has been about the skills and knowledge to coach your clients. How about yourself? Who is your coach?

It is an excellent idea to have a coach of your own. This way you demonstrate the importance of coaching. You take it seriously and you model that for your clients. Also, you can coach yourself by giving yourself the same care and attention that you give your clients. This is one way you can ensure you are at your best for your clients.

When you are a coach you are also a leader. A leader has three main attributes:

↓ skill
↓ knowledge
↓ providing an example

This book will give you skill and knowledge, and you are also a role model for your clients, so you provide an example of what coaching can do. If there is a difference between what you say and what you do, clients will pay more attention to what you do.

A coach develops in three dimensions:

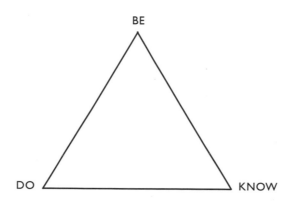

- First, you have skill; you are able to act, to make a difference. You grow on the left-hand side by what you can *do*.
- Secondly, you learn more, you have more knowledge, you expand on the right-hand side by what you *know*.
- Lastly, and most importantly, you grow on the top by providing a model for the client by who you can *be*. You become more of the person that you really want to be, you are comfortable with yourself, you have your dreams, you have your goals and values, and you work with them. Your coaching is part of living your values. This gives your life an aesthetic aspect. Every life can be a work of art. Some are paintings, some are music and some are sculptures. When your life is balanced, it has artistic appeal. It is a fusion of conscious and unconscious. It is precious.

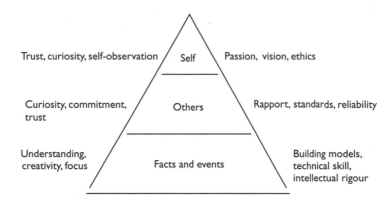

Building on these distinctions, a coach needs to develop themselves in three different domains:

- On the left in the figure are the qualities of looking inwards – how the coach treats themselves.
- The first domain, at the top, is the domain of identity. This is about self-management. As a coach you need to trust yourself. This means knowing that you are living your own ethics and that you have the ability to carry out your promises.
- On the right are the qualities in relation to others. A good coach is curious about others. Human behaviour is fascinating – even when people make horrendous mistakes. How can people make such mistakes one day and do things so well the next? What would it be like if your best became your average?

With curiosity goes passion. It is not the curiosity of a visitor to a museum, but the curiosity of an explorer looking for treasure. A coach also has vision – vision in the sense of being able to see the best that is in everyone, however obscured, vision in the sense of looking forward to a better world where people are able to fulfil their potential and the part that they can play in such a world.

The second domain, marked in the middle of the triangle, is the domain of relationships. A good coach has rapport with themselves. They are comfortable with themselves. They know their goals and values and boundaries. They stand by their ethics. They know that all their actions not only affect others but also themselves, so they take care. Ethics are their internal standards. They are also reflected in their external standards, the level of skill and attention they show towards others. As coaching becomes a recognized profession, so professional standards will be expected more and more.

The third domain (at the bottom of the triangle) is the domain of facts and events. The coach knows their subject and understands it. They are able to be creative within it, blending different approaches to create something new, depending on the circumstances. They are also good at building models of their processes for others to understand, with expertise and intellectual rigour. Their work is respected.

What this adds up to is that a good coach knows themselves. They will be clear about their goals and the values behind the goals, they will have made their action plans and as far as possible be living the values of their goals. They have their boundaries. They will not take clients if they feel that they are not the best person to be their coach or if the client needs someone else. If, for example, after an initial session a coach decides that it is more important for a client to see a medical doctor, they will say so and postpone the coaching relationship until the client has done so. Sometimes a client will need a therapist and the coach should refer them to one if they can recommend one. In fact, it is a good idea for a coach to know a good medical doctor as well as a number of trustworthy complementary therapists, psychologists consultants, osteopaths, trainers and counsellors, so they can refer the client if necessary.

A coach will respect the beliefs and values of their clients, but be clear about their own. They will not take any client they feel uncomfortable with. Sometimes a client will be talking about an emotional issue and the coach will find it difficult to deal with because they too are dealing with that issue. In that case, it can be a good idea to tell the client about this and explain that you need some time to deal with that issue yourself before you can help the client with it.

There is the story of a woman who took her son to Gandhi and asked him to tell the boy to stop eating sugar. It was bad for him and he was eating too much. Gandhi was a hero for the boy and his mother knew that if he told him to stop eating sugar then he would listen to him.

'Bring him back in a week,' said the holy man.

In a week the woman brought back her son.

'Give up sugar,' said Gandhi directly to the boy.

'The boy went away and the mother asked, 'Why did you ask me to bring him back in a week?'

'Last week I was still eating sugar,' replied Gandhi.

SELF-OBSERVATION AND SELF-DEVELOPMENT

Self-observation is an integral part of coaching yourself. Many coaches have a habit of meditation or set aside a regular time every day when they relax and review the day. A good coach is curious about themselves and how good they can be.

Here are some questions that are worth answering about yourself and your coaching work:

↓　'Why am I coaching?'

↓　'What am I learning about others and myself in my coaching?'

↓　'What makes me uncomfortable when I am coaching?'

↓　'What do I find hard to understand about people in my coaching work?'

↓　'What does that tell me about myself?'

↓　'What beliefs of mine are being challenged?'

↓　'What am I learning about my relationships with people?'

↓　'When am I most effective in coaching?'

↓　'Am I providing a role model for my clients of the qualities I am asking from them?'

These questions are worth reflecting on, not just once but as a continual reflection to develop yourself and your skills as a coach.

Traps for Coaches

There are some traps that can snare you in coaching. Watch out for the following:

↓　'I have to make a difference in every session.'
You do not. This is pressure to perform and will get in the way of coaching. You *will* make a difference in every session; you *can* make a difference in every session. You do not *have to*. Nor can you control the difference you make, because only the client can measure that.

↓　'The client has to like me.'
No, they do not. Many clients will like you; many might be your friends in other circumstances. But they do not have to like you. What is needed between coach and client is a professional relationship based on rapport and trust.

↓　'I am responsible for the client in some way.'
You are not. You do not have to take care of the client. You are not their parent. Nor do they have to take care of you. You are not their child. The client has responsibility for their own life. If they try to give it to you, just respectfully hand it back.

↓   'I have to share the problem and feel with the client.'

No, you do not, though rapport and second position will allow you to understand the client better. There are two types of second position. One is cognitive. When you have good rapport and a cognitive second position with the client, you will understand their world and how they think. This is invaluable in coaching. There is also an emotional second position. This will allow you to feel what the client is feeling. It can be useful to feel a little of what the client is feeling, but do not enter into that feeling. It is the client's feeling, not yours. Also, you do not need to share their problem, even if it has some resonance for you. It is the client's problem.

↓   'I have to know something of the client's business to do business coaching.'

Not necessarily. The client knows about their business. What you need to know in order to coach them is their view and experience of their business. Of course it is useful for the client to tell you about their part in the business, but you would need to know that in any case, however knowledgeable you were about the business. You may want to do some prior research by visiting the company's website, reading their brochures and buying their products. Yet it can be an advantage not knowing about the business, because then you can ask some very simple questions without thinking that you already know the answers. You can ask the best sort of naïve questions – those that question the basis of what the client is doing and why the client is doing it. If you do have some knowledge of the business, it may blind you rather than enlighten you. You may assume things that are not true and prior knowledge may make you less curious about the client's experience.

↓   'I must not confront the client.'

You may confront the client if they are avoiding an issue. Clients may talk round and round in circles and you may want to get to the bottom line. So you may have to interrupt the client and say something like 'Excuse me, I think there is an important issue underneath this that has not yet surfaced. Can I tell you what I think is behind what you are saying?' If this is done with rapport, the client will agree. You should forewarn the client about this sort of bottom lining in the initial session when you manage the client's expectations, and should ask them if they agree. Once you have permission, it will not be a problem. The coach is an ally to the client's best self, and the client's best self is served by honesty and confronting an issue if necessary. That does not mean that the coach has to rub the client's nose in every issue. The coach may well decide there is an issue behind what the client is saying, but now is not the time to confront it.

↓   'I have to keep control of the coaching process.'

You cannot keep control of the coaching process, so do not even try. The client has the control, if anyone has it. However, control is not a very good way to think about it anyway. Control is a mechanical metaphor and coaching is about human beings trying to understand each other, with the best intentions. There can be no control.

Finally, some more traps for the coach to avoid:

↓ *One-upping*. One temptation is for the coach to try to keep control by one-upping the client. Whatever the client does or achieves, the coach tops it by telling about their achievements. However, coach and client are not in competition. The client owns their results. Coaches differ a great deal in how much they disclose about themselves. Some opt for an almost psychoanalytical detachment, others are prepared to disclose a lot about their life. Most coaches fall in between, but if they do tell the client about their own experience, there is always a reason, and that reason is to help the client.

↓ *Judging*. Coaches need to respect the client, but not judge them. Once a coach judges, they cease to understand. However, coaches have their own boundaries and are free to stop working with a client if they lose respect for that client.

↓ *Psychoanalysing*. You do not need to understand the past to design the future. Nor do you need to explain client behaviour in terms of unconscious forces for them to take action to change their life. Many clients have a great deal of cognitive understanding about their predicament but remain stuck firmly in it. Coaching clients will be taking action to move on, whatever their cognitive understanding.

↓ *Commanding*. Coaches can make suggestions, sometimes strongly, but they can never tell the client what to do. Many clients will ask for advice, but coaches do not give advice. They connect the client with their goals and values so the client can direct themselves.

TOWARDS MASTERY

Learning can be divided into four main stages:

↓ *Unconscious incompetence*. You don't know and you don't know you don't know. Once upon a time, you did not know about coaching. Then you learned about it, got interested and moved onto the next stage.

↓ *Conscious incompetence*. You started to practise and to learn, you knew you were learning and you knew your shortcomings.

↓ *Conscious competence*. Now you are good. You know what you are doing and your skills are habitual and consistent.

↓ *Unconscious competence*. Now your skill is automatic. This is the aim of learning. If you have reached this stage in your coaching, then congratulations!

However, the different skills of coaching may be at different levels, for example a coach may be unconsciously competent at questions, but still be at the stage of conscious competence with regard to rapport.

↓ *Then there is mastery. Mastery is more than unconscious competence, it has an extra aesthetic dimension — it is effective and also beautiful to watch. You know when you are watching a master, although you may not appreciate their skill because they make everything look easy. When you have reached mastery, you no longer have to try, everything comes together in a constant flow; you enter a 'flow state'. It is as if things happen by themselves. This takes time and effort to achieve, but the results are magical.*

We want this book to be a significant part of your achieving mastery in coaching.

SUMMARY

A coach is a leader. They develop in three dimensions:
  1 *What they can do*
  2 *What they know*
  3 *Who they are*

A coach also develops their skills in
    self-mastery
    relationships
    facts and events

Coaches should avoid the traps of thinking that:
    They have to make a difference in every session.
    The client has to like them.
    They are responsible for the client in some way.
    They have to share the client's problem.
    They need to know something of the client's business.
    They must not confront the client.
    They have to keep control of the coaching process.

Coaches do not:
    try to be one up on the client
    judge the client
    psychoanalyse the client
    direct the client

Mastery is within your grasp. Take it!

ACTION STEPS

1 **Set aside 10 minutes every day to relax or meditate. Either follow a meditative tradition (e.g. Transcendental Meditation) or simply relax and concentrate on your breathing. Whenever your attention strays, just notice that it has strayed and come back to focusing on your breathing. This practice teaches focus and concentration and is deeply relaxing.**

2 **Set aside five minutes at the end of each day to review one habit.**
> **Where does this habit seem to come from?**
> **What does it accomplish?**
> **What triggers it?**
> **What do you feel about it?**

3 **Do a stocktake of yourself as a coach (*see Resources, page 196*). This will give you a comprehensive picture of all your resources. You can also use this stocktake as a task for clients.**

4 **Who are you when you are a coach? What is your metaphor as a coach?**
> **An explorer?**
> **An awakener?**
> **A dancer?**
> **A musician?**
> **A sculptor?**
> **Why did you choose this metaphor?**

5 **Review the questions about happiness (*page 9*).**
> **What do you need to be happy?**
> **What do you get from this?**
> **What is important about this?**
> **What are you doing to achieve these things?**
> **What is stopping you?**

Compare your answers to those you wrote down earlier. What has changed?

⇨ THE DREAM ENDS

⇨ ⇨ ⇨ We walk to the centre of the cathedral and look up in wonder. The darkness stretches far into the distance. The light coming through the doors is becoming weaker as the daylight starts to die.

We walk out and do not look back.

Outside everything is still the same. People are doing the same things that they were doing before.

There is a loud noise. Toc! Toc!

There is an old man, hammer in hand, driving nails into three pieces of timber. He looks frail and we walk over. His face is like rock beaten by the sea, very strong but marked by time, salt, wind and waves. His eyes are deep blue and hiding behind tired eyelids. He is wearing a very old sweater, made by a past lover when he was young. Now it is hanging on his small and fragile body.

'What are you doing, mister?'

He doesn't answer, just hammers the next nail into a piece of wood. On that wood is written: 'Danger!'

We move closer and whisper in his ear, 'What are you doing, mister?'

He lifts his head and looks directly at us. His eyes show worry and concern.

'What?'

'This?'

'My daughter is pregnant. I'm afraid the little boy could hurt himself, so before I leave this world I need to warn him… I will teach him the word "danger" so he will remember and stay safe!'

He smiles into the distance.

'Did you put some danger signs in the cathedral?'

'Of course, my dear! Especially on those steps. I saw how children run up and down there. I don't want my grandson to hurt himself… It's very dangerous!'

'Thank you very much, mister.'

He smiles again.

We run back into the cathedral, jump over the signs and run up the stairs. Thinking about children running up and down, we laugh at ourselves – we were so afraid without knowing why.

We arrive at the top of the stairs, move a heavy curtain that is covering a big door and see that the sun is starting to rise in a flurry of gold, silver, purple and other colours for which there are no words.

We look down and see the woman talking with the old man. He gives her a sign and they both sit down to talk.

In a few minutes he is sleeping in her arms. She puts his head on a comfortable pillow and stands up. She looks sideways at us and we wave to her.

She turns off the lamp and walks away, smiling hugely.

We will remember her.

PART IV

RESOURCES

GENERAL COACHING RESOURCES

ETHICS AND STANDARDS

The following is a set of pragmatic ethics and standards developed by the International Coaching Community.

This code provides the broad principles to which the ICC subscribes. Principles are a code of action that guides behaviour based on values.

The principles are based on Common Law; in other words, they do not lay down in detail what the coach must do, but give guiding principles within which the coach can move freely.

Because we are interdependent with others, every action has two consequences: a consequence for others and a consequence for ourselves. Every action changes us as well as the world.

Ethics are the principles of action that you apply to yourself. Therefore ethics cannot be imposed from the outside. The reward or sanction for ethics is in the actions themselves.

Standards cover the principles of actions that apply to others. They are the visible results of your actions as they affect others. Some ethical principles also have implications for standards, in that if you act unethically, you will also harm others or act against their interests and this will be visible.

Ethics and standards are built on the presuppositions of coaching. Coaches act as if these are true in their coaching:

↓   There is no failure, only feedback.
    Failure is only a judgement about short-term results. A client never fails.
↓   If you want to understand, act.
    Action is the answer. The learning is in the doing.
↓   We already have all the resources we need or can create them.

There are no unresourceful clients, only unresourceful states of mind. The client's deeper wisdom is waiting to be discovered.

↓   All behaviour has a purpose.

Actions are not random; clients are always trying to achieve something, although they may not be clear what that is.

↓   Having a choice is better than having no choice.

If clients are given a better choice according to their values and beliefs, then they will take it.

↓   You are doing the best you can.

And you could probably do better.

↓   You create your own reality.

Clients operate as if the mental maps they create are reality. These mental maps can limit their potential more than any real constraints from the outside world.

↓   Coaching is an equal, synergistic partnership.

If you think one and one only make two, it is only because you have forgotten the power of the 'and'.

↓   The client has the answers.

The coach has the questions.

ETHICAL PRINCIPLES

1. Trust

At the heart of every coaching relationship is trust. The client must trust the coach for coaching to work at its best. Trust is built over time; the coach must show themselves to be trustworthy.

To be trustworthy, the coach needs to demonstrate competence and integrity.

Competence

The coach acts to the best of their ability with every client.

The coach demonstrates the core competencies (see *page 166*).

The coach makes effort to stay updated with developments in coaching methodology.

The coach is aware of their level of skills and always works to improve those skills.

A coach is aware of their own personal problems and ensures that they do not adversely affect their professional coaching relationship with their clients. If necessary, they will obtain professional help at an early stage, either from another coach or from an appropriate professional. If these problems are causing difficulties in dealing with their clients, they will consider limiting or terminating their coaching activities.

Integrity

The coach acts consistently, honours agreements and keeps promises.
The coach keeps the client's material confidential except where otherwise authorized by the client or required by law.

2. Respect for the Client

The coach will treat clients with dignity and respect.
The coach will never take advantage of the client personally, sexually or financially.
The coach will obtain permission from any client before using their names or endorsements as references.
The coach will not seek to impose their own beliefs, values or views on the client.

3. Honesty

The coach will be aware of their level of skills and qualifications and will advertise, market and present them in an honest way.
The coach will only accept clients where they perceive a match between the client's needs and their own skills.

4. Professional Respect

The coach will not do anything that harms the general understanding or acceptance of coaching as a profession.
The coach will not claim or imply outcomes for coaching that they cannot congruently assert.

STANDARDS OF THE ICC

These guidelines are for all professional members of the ICC. They prescribe minimum standards of practice to be followed by coaches when they provide their professional services as members of the ICC.

1. Competence

↓ Coaches will give their best skills to each of their clients, and demonstrate the core competencies in their coaching.

↓   They will strive to be aware of current best business practices, new technologies, legal requirements and standards as related to the coaching profession.

↓   They will seek to improve and expand their skills through reading, peer contact and training.

↓   Coaches will always be aware of their skills, their strengths and their limitations. They will only accept work that they believe themselves competent to perform.

↓   Coaches will not make claims that they cannot congruently assert. Nor will they claim any skills, credentials or qualifications that they do not hold, nor knowingly allow others to claim them on their behalf, either in written documents or verbal statements.

2. Respect for Clients

↓   Coaches will respect the rights of others to hold differing opinions and beliefs from their own. They will not attempt to present their own beliefs, values or opinions as correct.

↓   At the beginning of the relationship, the coach will ensure as far as possible that the client understands the coaching agreement between them.

↓   Coaches will not unfairly discriminate against clients on any basis.

↓   Coaches will not take advantage of the client personally, sexually or financially.

↓   The coach will obtain permission from any client before using their names or endorsements as references.

↓   The coach will honour all agreements and keep their promises to clients.

3. The Profession of Coaching

↓   Coaches will respect the rights of others in copyrights, intellectual property, trademarks and patents. They will acknowledge the contributions of others where appropriate.

↓   Coaches will not willingly engage in any activity that could bring the profession of coaching into disrepute. If they learn of misuse or misrepresentation of their work, they will take reasonable steps to correct it.

4. Confidentiality and Conflict of Interest

↓   The coach will keep the client's material confidential except where otherwise authorized by the client, required by law or for other compelling reasons such as imminent harm to others. This material may be verbal in face-to-face session or via technology such as telephone, computers or voicemail.

↓   Wherever possible a coach will not take on professional obligations where pre-existing relationships could create a conflict of interest. If such a conflict arises, the coach will aim to resolve it within the framework of the ethical guidelines and standards.

↓   Coaches may use client material, in training and written material, provided the client is in no way identifiable.

↓ The coach will disclose to client all fees that they receive from third parties as a result of referrals or advice they give concerning that client.

↓ Where professionally appropriate, coaches may co-operate with other professionals to help their client, always with the client's permission.

↓ When the coach is asked to provide services to a person or organization at the request of a third party, they will carefully evaluate the relationship between the two and determine that there is no conflict of interest with regard to the coach's differing roles or issues of confidentiality.

↓ In cases where a coach's employer is the same as that of their client (for example when a business engages and pays a coach to coach one or more people in the business), a coach will clarify in advance with both client and employer the feedback given to the employer, the form it will take and the results that the employer wants, thereby ensuring advance agreement between coach, client and employer and that the confidentiality or trust of the client is not breached. If no agreement can be reached, the coach will decline the work.

5. Feedback and Progress

↓ Coaches will take reasonable steps to measure their clients' progress. If the client is not progressing, they will discuss this openly with the client as part of the coaching relationship.

↓ Coaches will create and keep adequate record of their work with clients to meet professional and legal requirements.

↓ Coaches will refer clients to other professionals when relevant, such as a counsellor, therapist or doctor when they know of a problem that needs such treatment.

↓ Coaches always seek to avoid harm or danger to themselves, clients or others in their work.

↓ When there is an interruption to the coaching, the coach will make reasonable efforts to make other arrangements for the client. If the interruption is a long one, this may involve finding the client an interim coach.

↓ The coaching relationship will be terminated by agreement between coach and client, usually at the end of a prepaid contract. If the coaching is terminated by the coach before the end of such a contract, they will offer to repay any fees paid in advance for coaching services not supplied. If the coaching is terminated by the client before the end of such a contract, the client will pay fees in lieu of notice if previously agreed.

6. Fees

↓ The coach will clearly inform the client about the logistics, fees and scheduling of the coaching relationship.

↓ A coach is free to charge whatever fee they want. They will disclose these fees at the beginning of the coaching relationship.

↓ If there is a problem with the payment of fees, the coach will take reasonable steps to discuss this with the client and agree a payment plan. If the client does not pay the agreed fees, the coach can take appropriate legal measures to collect them.

CORE COACHING COMPETENCIES

These are the key competencies that coaches need to demonstrate to become certified by the Lambent do Brasil International Coaching Certification and join the International Coaching Community. These are also the skills that they will demonstrate consistently in their professional coaching work.

General

1 Understands and follow the ethical guidelines and the published standards of the International Coaching Community.
2 Makes a clear distinction between content and process of the client's issue, that is, *what* the issue is and *how* the client represents it.
3 Works always to give the client more choices than they presently have.

Knowledge

1 The background of coaching.
2 What distinguishes coaching from counselling, therapy, training and consulting.
3 Familiarity with the specialist vocabulary of coaching.
4 The criteria for testing both process and outcome goals.

Skills

Relationship

1 Builds a relationship of respect and trust with the client.
2 Works so the client is accountable for the coaching process and the tasks they agree to in that process.
3 Creates an equal, synergistic partnership with the client.

Listening

1   Is fully present and attentive during the coaching process, listening and supporting the client's self-expression, focusing on the client's agenda and not their own.
2   Is in touch with and pays attention to their intuition.

Self-management

1   Keeps their own perspective and does not become enmeshed in the client's emotions.
2   Evaluates and distinguishes the different messages the client gives.
3   Is sensitive to and calibrates the client's non-verbal signals.

Enquiries and Questions

1   Helps the client to define the present situation in detail.
2   Asks powerful questions that provoke insight, discovery and action.
3   Provides clear and articulate feedback.
4   Uses different perspectives to reframe and clarify the client's experience.
5   Supports the client's growing self-awareness.
6   Makes the client aware of incongruence between their thoughts, emotions and actions.

Feedback

1   Shows the client areas of strength and elicits and supports their resources.
2   Shows the client where habits are holding them back and supports any change they want to make.
3   Celebrates the client's successes.

Goals, Values and Beliefs

1   Works with the client to overcome limiting beliefs.
2   Explores the client's values and makes the client aware of them.
3   Does not impose their own values.
4   Works with the client to clarify their goals and check that they are congruent with their values.
5   Clearly requests actions that will lead the client towards their goals.

Designing Action Plans and Tasks

1   Creates opportunities for ongoing learning for the client.

2   Gives appropriate tasks for the client to challenge them and move them forward towards their goals.

3   Helps the client to develop an appropriate, measurable action plan with target dates.

4   Provides challenges to take the client beyond their perceived limitations.

5   Holds the client accountable for the mutually agreed tasks and actions.

RESOURCES FOR CHAPTER 2

COACHING DEFINITIONS

Coaching shares a broad approach and has some similarities with training, teaching, consultancy, counselling, therapy and mentoring. However, there are crucial differences too:

↓ *Counselling* usually works remedially on a client's problems. The client usually feels uncomfortable or dissatisfied with their life.

↓ *Therapy* is for a client who seeks relief from psychological and/or physical symptoms. The client wants emotional healing.

The client's motive in therapy or counselling is usually to get away from pain or discomfort rather than moving towards desired goals. Both therapy and counselling are likely to involve understanding and working with past experience.

↓ *Training* is the process of acquiring knowledge or skills by study and experience. The trainer is usually the expert; they know or can do something the student cannot. Training is usually one to many rather than one to one.

↓ *Teaching* is similar to training in that the teacher knows something the student does not and the student learns directly. The learner has the questions; the teacher has the answers.

Training and teaching are similar to coaching in that they usually focus on skills, but the approach is different. The student learns directly from the teacher or trainer.

↓ *Consultancy.* A consultant has the expertise to solve business problems and usually deals with the overall business or specific parts of it, not with the individuals within it.

A consultant may recommend coaching for individuals as part of the business package.

↓ *Mentoring.* A mentor is a senior colleague who gives advice and provides a role model. Mentoring is not so goal-focused as coaching and the discussions will be wide-ranging. A mentor usually has a lot of experience in the client's field of business.

COACHING

Approach to problem
Generative

Remedial
therapy
counselling

Effect on the whole business
Indirect

Direct
consultancy

Time focus
Present and future

Past
therapy
counselling

Role
Asks questions

Gives answers
training
teaching

Approach through
Action

Understanding
therapy
counselling

Experience in the client's business
Unnecessary but useful

Essential
mentoring

Numbers
One to one
(although there is also team coaching)

One to many

training
teaching

Direction
Non-directive

Directive
managing

Here is an example of the different possible approaches to get a solution.

Elizabeth was an outstanding salesperson and was promoted to sales manager. Now instead of selling, she is managing her colleagues. She takes over her new position and wonders how she will tell them what to do. She knows how to sell, but not to manage. She does not feel confident that being good at sales makes her a good manager. She knows that she will get some enthusiastic support, some cautious co-operation and some downright hostility. She does not know how to start approaching her colleagues. She wants help.

A counsellor would guide Elizabeth with advice and work directly with the stress she feels. They would not know anything about Elizabeth's work except what she tells them. They would work on her confidence and self-belief. They would not directly try to make her more competent at her job or give her techniques to get on with her colleagues.

If Elizabeth was upset, stressed, couldn't sleep, felt anxious and could not cope with the new work, she might consider therapy. The therapist would work with her to remove the stress then to open alternative ways of working so she did not feel so stressed. The therapist might also look into her past life for reasons why she is stressed or lacked confidence in this situation.

If Elizabeth was not feeling stressed, she might consider training or teaching. She could learn specific management or communication skills to help her in her new position. She might attend a training class targeted on her specific needs with an expert on these skills.

She might be assigned a mentor, a senior manager who would meet her, talk over her new challenges and advise her in the light of their experience what might be best to do in her situation.

Lastly, she might talk to a consultant to explore how her department could be restructured or how her department and responsibilities fitted within the organization as a whole. He might advise training or coaching for her or for other members of her department.

A coach would work with her in a different way. While acknowledging Elizabeth's stress, the coach would work with her to increase her confidence, get her to set goals for both her interpersonal skills and her self-confidence, and find out what was important to her in her working life. They would explore any limiting beliefs she had about herself and others and give her specific tasks to test her concerns and to learn from the challenges she faced.

The coach would not give Elizabeth advice or tell her what to do, or look for reasons in her past life, but might discuss with her how others react to her, her part in provoking those reactions and how she could get on better with others in her new role. Her tasks might include sitting down with all her staff individually and having an informal chat to get to know their concerns. Together, Elizabeth and her coach might explore how she could ask good questions to get the information she needed and how to listen to the replies. The next action step might be to send out a memo (handwritten), thanking them for their time and commenting on one specific thing they mentioned. Elizabeth might also talk over with her coach how to 'manage upwards': to talk over her plans with her supervisor, to ask questions that get good feedback. If she intends to make some changes then they need to be thoroughly discussed. Then she needs to tell people what she wants to do and why. She may need coaching on her rapport skills. The coaching would mobilize her resources, boost her confidence, clarify her goals and help her with specific skills to implement the changes she wants to make.

Finally a coach would take a leaf from the consultant's book and explore the system in which she works. What support is she getting from her department? How does it support her? Does it make it harder for her? A person can only do their best in the system they are in. One part of the coaching could be changing departmental procedures to allow her to work more easily.

RESOURCES FOR CHAPTER 3

GOALS

Coaching is exploring the present and designing the future. The first step to designing the future is to give yourself direction by setting long-term goals.

Some clients may be resistant to setting long-term goals because they are afraid they will be disappointed or they feel it undermines their spontaneity. The answer to both these objections is that goals do not tie you down and you are perfectly able to change them at any time. They do not stop your spontaneity at any moment.

Everyone has the goal of having a happy and fulfilled life, whatever this may mean to them. Long-term goal setting is just getting a little more specific about that happiness and fulfilment.

Your Life Goals

Set between four and seven long-term goals for your life. These should be well in the future, at least ten years ahead.

Do not rank them in order – all will be important and will work together synergistically.

Use the wheel of life to help you set these goals. You do not need to set a goal for every part of the wheel, but between them the goals should cover the following parts of your life:

love, relationships, friendships and family
leisure and fun
money
work and profession
health
contribution and spiritual life

Because these goals are in the far future, they may not be very specific and they may seem fanciful at the moment. Express them in very simple, positive language, in other words what you want to achieve, *not* what you want to avoid. They do not have to be specific and you do not know yet if they are achievable.

Think about the following questions:

What do you want to achieve in ten years' time?
What do you want to look back on?
What do you want to have achieved when you reach the end of your life?
What is truly important *to you*?

Goal 1

Goal 2

Goal 3

Goal 4

Goal 5

Goal 6

Notes

Five-year Goals

Take your list of long-term life goals (ten-year goals).

Take each goal and set goals that you need to accomplish *in five years* in order to be on track with those long-term goals.

What are the intermediate steps you need to take?

Where will you be and what do you need to have accomplished in five years?

Goal 1: Five-year intermediate goals

Goal 2: Five-year intermediate goals

Goal 3: Five-year intermediate goals

Goal 4: Five-year intermediate goals

Goal 5: Five-year intermediate goals

Goal 6: Five-year intermediate goals

Two-year Goals

Take your list of five-year goals.

Take each goal and set goals that you need to accomplish in the *next two years* in order to be on track with those five-year goals.

What are the steps you need to take?

Where will you be and what do you need to have accomplished in two years?

Goal 1: Two-year intermediate goals

Goal 2: Two-year intermediate goals

Goal 3: Two-year intermediate goals

Goal 4: Two-year intermediate goals

Goal 5: Two-year intermediate goals

Goal 6: Two-year intermediate goals

One-year Goals

Take your list of two-year life goals.

Take each goal and set goals that you need to accomplish in the *next year* in order to be on track with those two-year goals.

What are the immediate steps you need to take?

Where will you be and what do you need to have accomplished in the next year?

Goal 1: One-year immediate goals

Goal 2: One-year immediate goals

Goal 3: One-year immediate goals

Goal 4: One-year immediate goals

Goal 5: One-year immediate goals

Goal 6: One-year immediate goals

 RESOURCES FOR CHAPTER 4

There are many ways to coach, and coaches must decide most of these for themselves. They will depend on the country, the type of coaching and the personality of the coach. Here are some ideas of what is possible and what many coaches do already.

How often will you meet?

Coaching should take place on a regular basis to maintain continuity and keep the client committed and motivated. Some coaches work with one face-to-face session a week. Others work only over the telephone, perhaps one half-hour session a week. Many coaches use a flexible mixture of the two, perhaps one session of one hour or two hours a month with a half-hour telephone conversation each week between the meetings.

Some coaches (particularly career coaches) devote a whole day to the initial meeting.

Many business coaches plan around a very open-ended schedule to suit their clients. They will agree to supply 12 hours coaching in three months and the client and coach schedule this according to their other commitments. This suits busy executives who may not be able to find time for a meeting for some weeks, but then be able to devote two or three hours in one day.

What form will the coaching take?

Coaching can take place either face to face, over the telephone, through video conferencing or by e-mail. Most coaches use a mixture of these, but face to face and telephone are best. Video conferencing needs the video facilities with both coach and client.

Geography also plays a part. When the client lives a long way away, telephone coaching will play a more dominant role.

E-mail coaching is the most difficult. It is very time-consuming, because the coach has to write the e-mails with care. E-mail coaching loses all the information that the coach can obtain through the body language of face-to-face sessions and the voice tone of telephone sessions. Also, it does not take place in real time. Some coaches are prepared to give e-mail back-up if it is important (say the client meets an unexpected difficulty and cannot talk to the coach on the telephone), but consistent e-mail coaching is one of the least satisfactory coaching methods.

Where will the coaching take place?

Most coaches prefer to have the client visit their office for a face-to-face meeting.

Coaching in the client's working environment is more difficult because all the work anchors are there to distract them.

Many coaches are prepared to travel to visit the client. This makes more sense if they are coaching a number of people at the same site for a business or doing team coaching in a business.

How much to charge?

This is difficult to specify; it varies from country to country and from area to area. Also, business coaches command higher fees than life coaches. Some coaches are prepared to be flexible about charges within reason, but coaching is a highly skilled profession and can make an enormous difference to an individual or business, so coaches are entitled to charge a fair fee, in line with training and consultancy rates in the area in which they work. Some coaches charge by the hour, some will charge per month, others for a three or six-month contract. Some will charge a business a percentage of the extra revenue that it makes as a result of the coaching. If the coach does this, then the contract needs to specify exactly how the results will be measured.

Over what time scale should the coaching take place?

Many coaches take clients on for a three-month period. At the end of that period, they will review the results and extend the coaching for another three months as necessary. Some coaches provide coaching in 10, 12 or 15-hour packages that can be taken up during the course of three or six months. Sometimes the issue is an urgent one and the coaching is intensive over two or three weeks until the issue is resolved.

What if the client is late for a call or a session?

This needs to be agreed in the initial session. Sometimes the time is simply lost. Sometimes the coach will extend the session if possible, but if there is another call or session immediately afterwards, they will not be able to. They might make up the time on the next call or session.

What if the client misses a session or cancels at the last moment?

Again, coach and client should agree in the initial session what happens in these cases. Some coaches will make up the session at another time. Others will not. They have set aside the time and if the client is ill or has an urgent call on their time, it is unfortunate, but why should the coach suffer? The client needs to take the coaching session seriously, and if the coach is too understanding and free with making up sessions, the client may lose commitment and think that the coaching is not so important and can be set aside if something else comes up unexpectedly.

What sort of clients can you coach?

Some coaches specialize in business coaching, others in life coaching. Many do both. There are some specialist career coaches. Some coaches like to coach teams. Work with whoever you are comfortable working with. Some coaches will want to meet and work with the client's partner as well, if the coaching is going to be intensive and change the direction of the client's life.

What material can you give in the first session?

There are many possibilities, for example:

> A *coaching agreement* (if you use one). This defines the coach's and the client's responsibilities. It should be a professional document.
>
> A *mind map or some other explanatory material on coaching*. This should give an easy-to-understand summary of coaching and how it works.
>
> A *wheel of life to complete for the next session*. The wheel of life is an excellent first task for the client to complete (see page 182).
>
> A *statement of your standards and qualifications*. This builds your credibility and reassures the client. It forms the basis of trust in you and the coaching process.
>
> A *psychometric test*, if you use one. This may be one of the well-known tests, such as Birkman or MBTI, or a more informal one that you have constructed to use with clients. It should give information for the assessment and help you get to know the client better.
>
> A *transcript of the last session*. Some coaches write up or record each session and give the client a transcript or audiotape of the session. This can be extremely helpful for the client.

What about a signed agreement?

Some coaches operate with a signed agreement. This is a professional way to work – it sets out the terms and conditions and leaves the coach and client in no doubt about what to expect. Such an agreement should also cover what happens in the event of a dispute. No coach should use a signed agreement with a client unless they have had it drawn up by a lawyer or solicitor who is familiar with coaching.

An agreement should cover the following points at the very least:

the coaching service the coach provides and the coach's responsibilities
the client's responsibilities
the fees and when they should be paid and what happens in the event of non-payment
the confidentiality of the client's material
what happens in the event of missing or cancelling a session by either coach or client
how long the coaching relationship will last and the terms of renewal
what happens in the event of a dispute or claim between coach and client
the period of notice that is needed for either party to terminate the coaching relationship

The agreement should be signed and dated, with a copy for both client and coach.

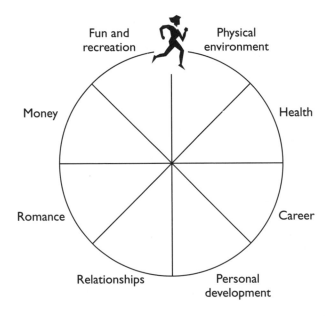

The wheel of life

THE DESIGNED ALLIANCE

Coaching is a partnership and it is important that coach and client discuss at the beginning what form it will take. This will help to manage the client's expectations and give the coach some valuable insights into how the client thinks. It also gives the message that the coach cares about how the client wants the coaching process to go. Also the client may have had an experience of coaching in the past and have some valuable feedback about what worked and what did not work. The following form may help with this.

How I Work Best with a Coach

Coaching works best for me, when the coach does these things:

Coaching works best for me, when the coach *avoids* doing these things:

ACCESSING CUES

We do not think just with our brain but with our whole body. We are a complete system of body and mind – it is not possible to think without affecting our bodies. We 'tune' our body into postures, gestures and breathing patterns to help us think in certain ways. The following signs are generalizations and not true in all cases.

	Visual	**Auditory**	**Kinaesthetic**
Eye accessing	Unfocused or up to the right or left.	In the midline.	Below the midline usually to the right.
Voice tone and tempo	Generally rapid speech, high clear voice tone.	Melodious tone, resonant, at a medium pace. Often has an underlying rhythm.	Low and deeper tonality, often slow and soft, with many pauses.
Breathing	High shallow breathing in the top part of the chest.	Even breathing in the middle part of the chest.	Deeper breathing from the abdomen.
Posture and gestures	More tension in the body, often with the neck extended. Often thinner (ectomorphic) body type.	Often medium (mesomorphic) body type. There may be rhythmic movements of the body as if listening to music. Head may be tilted to the side in thought in the 'telephone position' (hand resting on the ear).	Rounded shoulders, head down, relaxed muscle tone, may gesture to abdomen and midline.

Some people think mostly in language and abstract symbols. This way of thinking is often called 'digital'. A person thinking this way typically has an erect posture, often with the arms folded. Their breathing is shallow and restricted, speech is in a monotone and often clipped, and they talk typically in terms of facts, statistics and logical arguments.

EYE ACCESSING CUES

These are also called Lateral Eye Movements or LEM.

Visualisation

Visual constructed images

Visual remembered images

Constructed sounds

Remembered sounds

Kinesthetic
(Feelings and bodily sensations)

Auditory Digital
(Internal dialogue)

NB. This is as you look at another person

These eye patterns are the most common, though some left-handed people and a few right-handed people may have a reversed pattern: remembered images and sounds may be to the person's right-hand side, their feelings may be down to their left and their internal dialogue will be down to their right. This is *different* but still *normal*!

Don't assume you know a person's eye accessing cues – always test.

The easiest way to test for accessing cues is to ask a question about feelings. In everyday situations, you can do this in an easy and conversational way by asking how they are feeling and watch for the accessing cue. Although research is scarce, it seems that if a person accesses the feeling down to their right, then they will have the standard accessing pattern. If they access their feelings down to their left, then they will tend to have a reversed pattern, in other words remembered images and sounds will be on their right and constructed images and sounds will be on their left.

Other Eye Patterns

Blinking

We blink all the time – it is part of the natural mechanism for lubricating the eyes. Many people blink more when they think.

Certain accessing cues are avoided

This could mean that the person is systematically blocking visual, auditory or kinaesthetic information from consciousness, perhaps as a result of earlier trauma.

No obvious accessing cue

Are you sure? The client may be talking about such familiar and obvious topics that they do not need to access. To get the clearest accessing cues, ask questions that need some thought.

Immediate auditory internal dialogue in response to every question

The person may be first repeating the question and then accessing the answer. This is part of their habitual thinking strategy. You may even see their lips move as they do this.

Unusual accessing cues

Probably the result of the person making a synesthesia (a mixture of representational systems simultaneously).

The NLP pattern is a guide and a generalization – and like all generalizations will be untrue some of the time! Remember the answer is in the person in front of you, not in the theory.

SENSORY-BASED WORDS AND PHRASES

The Visual System

Visual Words

blank, clarify, colour, dark, focus, foresee, hazy, horizon, illusion, illustrate, imagination, insight, light, look, notice, outlook, perspective, picture, reflect, reveal, scene, see, shine, show, vision, visualize, watch

Visual Phrases

I see what you mean.
I am looking closely at the idea.
We see eye to eye.
I have a hazy notion.
He has a blind spot.
Show me what you mean.
You'll look back on this and laugh.
This will shed some light on the matter.
It colours his view of life.
It appears to me.
beyond a shadow of doubt
taking a dim view
The future looks bright.
The solution flashed before his eyes.
mind's eye
a sight for sore eyes

The Auditory System

Auditory Words

accent, acoustic, ask, audible, buzz, cackle, call, clear, click, comment, croak, cry, deaf, dialogue, discuss, dissonant, dumb, echo, growl, harmonious, harmony, hum, hush, listen, loud, melodious, monotonous, musical, mute, pitch, proclaim, question, quiet, remark, resonate, rhythm, ring, rumble, say, sigh, shout, shrill, silence, sound, speechless, squeak, tell, tone, tune, vocal, whine, whisper

Auditory Phrases

on the same wavelength
living in harmony
That's all Greek to me.
a lot of mumbo jumbo
turn a deaf ear
rings a bell
calling the tune
music to my ears
word for word
unheard of
clearly expressed
give an audience
hold your tongue
in a manner of speaking
loud and clear
The place was humming with activity.
a pronounced condition
The silence was eloquent.
The empty room shouted a warning.
a sizzling frying pan
a tumultuous reception
ping the internet site
a cacophony of colour
What you say chimes in with my own thinking on the subject.
There were subtle undertones to the remark.
It ended not with a bang, but with a whimper.

The Kinaesthetic System

(Including the Olfactory and Gustatory Systems)

Kinaesthetic Words

balance, break, cold, concrete, contact, feel, firm, gentle, grab, grasp, handle, hard, heavy, hit, hold, hot, jump, pressure, push, rough, rub, run, scrape, seize, sensitive, sharp, smooth, soft, solid, sticky, stress, stuck, suffer, tackle, tangible, tap, tension, tickle, tight, touch, vibrate, walk, warm

Kinaesthetic Phrases

I will get in touch with you.
I can grasp that idea.
I got the sharp end of her tongue.
Hold on a second.
surfing the Internet
I feel it in my bones.
There was tension in the air.
a warm-hearted man
a cool customer
The pressure was tremendous.
thick-skinned
a sticky predicament
scratch the surface
I can't put my finger on it.
going to pieces
control yourself
firm foundation
heated argument
not following the discussion
smooth operator
The project is up and running.
His voice had an edge to it.
breaking the mould
sweating it out
swallowing your pride
being stuck in the problem
He has a soft spot for her.
He needs a kick in the pants to get him working.

Olfactory Words

fishy, fragrant, fresh, musky, nosy, scented, smelly, smoky, sniff, stale

Gustatory Words

bitter, bland, chewy, flavour, gall, juicy, minty, mouthwatering, nauseous, salty, sour, spicy, succulent, sugary, sweet, taste, toothsome

Olfactory and Gustatory Phrases

smell a rat

a fishy situation

a bitter pill

fresh as a daisy

a taste for the good life

a sweet person

an acid comment

a nose for the business

eating humble pie

the smell of sanctity

a mouthwatering meal

Non-sensory-specific Words and Phrases

The majority of words have no sensory connotations at all. These are sometimes known as 'digital'. You can use them when you want to give the other person the choice to think in whatever representational system they wish.

Digital Words

assume, attend, change, choose, competence, condition, connection, conscious, consequence, consider, decide, evaluate, future, goal, idea, know, learn, logic, meditate, memory, model, motivate, outcome, past, present, process, program, recognize, remember, representation, resource, result, sequence, theory, thing, think, understand

 RESOURCES FOR CHAPTER 7

Certain

(I am completely certain about this belief.)

Important

(This is very important to my goal.)

Unimportant

(This is not at all important to my goal.)

Uncertain

(I am not at all certain about this belief.)

BELIEFS IN TIME

What are your beliefs about these subjects?

How have your beliefs changed?

If you have not reached a certain age, make a guess as to what your beliefs might be then.

Subject	Childhood	Age 15	Age 25	Age 35	Age 50	Age 65
Age						
Beauty						
Happiness						
Home						
Love						
Career						
Possibilities						

 RESOURCES FOR CHAPTER 8

EVERYDAY ANCHORS

Explore the anchors you respond to in your everyday life, both positive and negative. Look at both your personal and professional life.

	Anchor	Your response
Visual		
Auditory		
Kinaesthetic		
Olfactory and Gustatory		

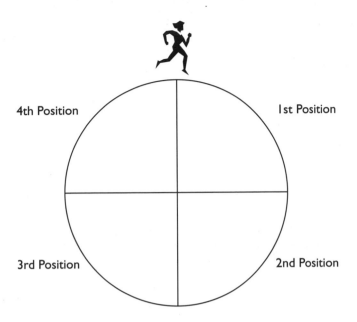

Wheel of Perspectives

 RESOURCES FOR CHAPTER 10

TAKING STOCK OF YOUR LIFE

Take some time to do a thorough stocktake of your life.

What skills do you have?

Think of every possible context.

What knowledge do you have?

Think of your education, specialist knowledge and what you have learned in the university of life.

Who do you know?

List all the people you know or have known – work colleagues or contacts, friends past and present, family, mentors and teachers, acquaintances, etc.

When you have finished, think how any or all of these could be resources for you as a coach.

 # GLOSSARY

Accountability: A key part of coaching. A client is accountable when they take responsibility for their actions. There are three key questions:

What are you going to do?

When will you do it?

How will you know you are successful?

Acknowledgement: Recognition of the client's identity or capability that allowed them to accomplish an important action or have an insight.

Anchor: A trigger – visual, auditory or kinaesthetic – that links with an action or emotional state.

Anchoring: The process of associating one thing with another.

Articulating: To succinctly sum up the client's experience in simple language. Another expression for clarifying.

As if: Using the imagination to explore the consequences of thoughts or actions 'as if' they had occurred when in fact they have not.

Backtrack: To review or summarize, using another person's key words, gestures and tonality.

Beliefs: The generalizations we make about others, the world and ourselves that become our operating principles. We act as if they were true and they become true for us.

Bottom lining: Putting the client's issue as clearly and precisely as possible, without losing any of the meaning.

Brainstorming: Generating ideas, alternatives, choices, perspectives or actions without judging first whether they are right or appropriate. There is no attachment to the ideas generated.

Break state: Using a movement or distraction to change an emotional state.

Calibration: Accurately recognizing another person's state by reading non-verbal signals.

Challenging: Stretching a client beyond their self-imposed limits by making a request.

Championing: When you champion a client, you stand up for them; you demonstrate you believe in them, even if they do not.

Clarifying: *See* Articulating.

Clearing: Making sure that a client's issues do not emotionally entangle you. Keeping yourself in a resourceful state even if a client is talking about issues that you also find difficult.

Client: The coach's partner in the alliance for change. The client wants to make changes. The client is responsible for the results. Coach and client together are responsible for the process.

Coach: The client's partner in the alliance for change. The coach assists the client to make the changes the client wants to make.

Coaching: Helping clients to examine what they do in the light of their intentions, helping them to take action that leads them to their goals, greater happiness and being able to express more of themselves.

Commitment: To take on a task without question, because it is emotionally and cognitively important.

Confidentiality: Information the client shares with the coach is not given to anyone else without the client's permission.

Congruence: The alignment of beliefs, values, skills and action, so that you 'walk your talk'. Congruence also means being in rapport with yourself.

Counselling: Working with a client who feels uncomfortable or dissatisfied with their life and is seeking guidance and advice. A counsellor works remedially on a client's problem.

Designing the alliance: Designing the partnership between coach and client. Designing the most beneficial way the coach can work with the client to forward their goals, vision and desired change.

Double loop coaching: Coaching that helps a client by dealing with their beliefs – changing the thinking that gave rise to the problem in the first place. (Also called generative coaching.)

Ecology: The overall consequences of your thoughts and actions in the total web of relationships in which you are part. There is also internal ecology: how a person's different thoughts and feelings fit together to make them congruent or incongruent (see Congruence).

Feedback: In the coaching situation, feedback is the response of the coach to what the client tells them, and the client's reaction to what the coach says. Feedback may be *reinforcing*, where it leads to more of the same behaviour, or *balancing*, where it leads to less of the behaviour, ultimately resulting in a change of behaviour.

First position: Perceiving the world from your own point of view. Being in touch with your own inner reality. One of four different perceptual positions.

Fourth position: Perceiving a situation from the point of view of the system in which it takes place, for example a family or a business.

Frame: A way of looking at something, a particular point of view, e.g. a negotiation frame looks at behaviour as if it were a form of negotiation.

Generative coaching: *See* Double loop coaching.

Goals: Desired results. Process goals are about the journey to the goal. Outcome goals are about the destination – the result.

Homework: Tasks, challenges or requests for the client to carry out. The client will report the results back to the coach at a mutually agreed time.

Incongruence: The state of being out of rapport with yourself, having an internal conflict which is expressed in behaviour. It may be sequential – for example, one action followed by another that contradicts it – or simultaneous – for example, saying you agree in a doubtful voice tone.

Internal dialogue: Talking to yourself.

Internal ecology: *See* Ecology.

Intuition: Inner knowledge that becomes available without conscious thought or rationale.

Life balance: The harmony of the client's relationship with the different parts of their life and its demands and how comfortable the client feels about that. Also the harmony of those commitments with each other.

Listening levels:

1   *Hearing*: Registering the sound of another person's voice.

2   *Listening to*: Hearing with a question in mind: 'What does this mean to me?' You are listening from inside your own experience.

3   *Listening for*: Having a preconceived idea and filtering and selecting from what the client says. You may make some judgements and may also have some internal dialogue.

4   *Conscious listening*: Deep listening with the minimum of judgement.

Mentoring: When a senior colleague in business, seen as more knowledgeable and worldly wise, gives advice and provides a role model. Mentoring involves wide-ranging discussions that may not be limited to the work context.

Metaphor: Indirect communication by a story or figure of speech implying a comparison. A metaphor implies overtly or covertly that one thing is like another. In NLP metaphor covers similes, stories, parables and allegories.

Mission: The direction and primary goal for a client.

Outcome goal: *See* Goal.

Perceptual Position: First, second, third and fourth position

Perspective: A particular viewpoint, for example first position (your own), second position (another person's) or third position (the relationship between the two). There are also many other perspectives, for example work, family, economics, politics, etc.

Preferred representational system: The representational system that a person typically uses to think consciously and organize their experience. It will appear particularly when the person is under stress.

Preframing: Setting up in advance what meaning you wish a client to give to your actions.

Presuppositions: Ideas or beliefs that are presupposed, i.e. taken for granted, and acted upon.

Process goal: *See* Goal.

Questions: A request for a response from a client. An opportunity for the client to find a response that furthers their goals and vision.

Rapport: A relationship of responsiveness to self or others.

Reframing: Understanding an experience in a different way, giving it a different meaning.

Representational systems: The different channels whereby we 're-present' information on the inside, using our senses: visual (sight), auditory (hearing), kinaesthetic (bodily sensation), olfactory (smell) and gustatory (taste).

Requesting: Asking a client to further their goals by taking a specific action.

Resources: Anything that can help you achieve an outcome, e.g. physiology, states, thoughts, beliefs, strategies, experiences, people, events, possessions, places, stories, etc.

Second position: Experiencing the point of view of another person.

Self-management: Looking after your own emotional state as a coach so you can be of maximum help to the client.

Single loop coaching: Coaching that helps a client without dealing with their beliefs.

Structures: Anchors designed to remind clients of their vision, goals, purpose or actions.

Therapy: Working with a client who seeks relief from psychological or physical symptoms. The client wants emotional healing and relief from mental pain.

Third position: Taking the viewpoint of a detached but resourceful single observer.

Transition: The point where you have let go of your old habits but have not yet consolidated the change or feel secure in the new habits. The most difficult time in the coaching process.

Trust: The feeling that you can rely on a person to fulfil their commitments. There are two elements of trust: sincerity and competence.

Values: Things that are important to you.

Vision: A combination of goals and values, the purpose and greater meaning in life.

BIBLIOGRAPHY

⇨ ⇨ ⇨ These are some useful books on coaching, NLP and the background to the kind of approach we have developed in this book.

Arendt, Hannah, *The Human Condition*, University of Chicago Press, 1958

Barrett, Richard, *Liberating the Corporate Soul*, Heinemann, 1998

Doyle, James S., *The Business Coach: A Game Plan for the New Work Environment*, John Wiley & Sons, 1999

Drucker, Peter, *The New Realities*, HarperCollins, 1989

Flaherty, James, *Coaching*, Butterworth-Heinemann, 1999

Fortgang, Laura, *Living your Best Life*, Thorsons, 2001

Gallwey, Timothy, *The Inner Game of Tennis*, Pan, 1986

—, *The Inner Game of Golf*, Pan, 1986

—, *The Inner Game of Work*, Texere, 1986

Goleman, Daniel, *Emotional Intelligence*, Bloomsbury, 1996

Hargrove, Roger, *Masterful Coaching*, Pfeiffer, 1995

Hemery, David, *What Makes a Champion?*, HarperCollins, 1991

Landsberg, Max, *The Tao of Coaching*, HarperCollins, 1999

Maturana, Humberto, and Varela, Francisco, *The Tree of Knowledge*, Shambhala, 1987

Morgan, Gareth, *Images of Organisation*, Sage, 1986

O'Connor, Joseph, *NLP and Sport*, Thorsons, 2001

—, *Leading with NLP*, Thorsons, 1998

—, *The NLP Workbook,* Thorsons, 2001

Ristad, Eloise, *A Soprano on her Head*, Real People Press, 1982

Tannen, Deborah, *You Just Don't Understand*, Ballantine Books, 1990

Whitmore, John, *Coaching for Performance*, Nicholas Brealey, 1996

Whitworth, Laura, *et al.*, *Co-active Coaching*, Davies-Black, 2001

LAMBENT DO BRASIL

Lambent do Brasil was founded by Andrea Lages and Joseph O'Connor and is based in São Paulo, Brazil.

We specialize in providing the best resources in coaching, training and consultancy to develop individuals and companies.

We are international specialists in business coaching. The company supplies coaching worldwide, both directly and through our partnerships and our international training programme for coaches. See our website www.lambentdobrasil.com

International Coaching Certification

We give our international coaching certification training worldwide and have trained hundreds of coaches from more than 15 countries. For details, *see*: www.lambentdobrasil.com.

We are founders of the Brazilian Association of Coaching, the Mexican Association of Coaching and the Swedish Association of Coaching. We were also trainers on the first training for the National Coaching Register in the UK, leading to a postgraduate degree in executive coaching from Derby University.

We are affiliated to the Scandinavian International University.

International Coaching Community (ICC)

The International Coaching Community has been created by Lambent do Brasil. It is a group of trained and qualified coaches who have passed successfully through the International Coaching Certification training. We continue to expand the Community through our training and our certified trainers. The Community has a shared commitment to quality, ethics and high standards in coaching. Visit the website: www.internationalcoachingcommunity.com

To find out more about the International Coaching Community and the International Coaching Certification, visit our website and contact: info@lambentdobrasil.com.

International Community of NLP (ICNLP)

ICNLP is an association for all who are interested in building an International Community of NLP based on the highest standards and ethics. It is open to all who are interested in NLP and offers a practitioner, a master practioner and a trainer training in NLP. For details see www.icnlp.org

Training Courses

Lambent do Brasil offers a variety of training courses to companies in:

coaching
sales
negotiation
systemic thinking
NLP and communications skills
leadership

All our courses are specially designed because every company is unique.

We specialize in systemic consultancy based on our systemic audit process, which analyses the culture and different systems of communication and management operating in the business.

Contact us for worldwide coaching, training and consultancy, including:

coaching certification training
executive and business coaching
systemic thinking training
systemic company analysis
practitioner, master practitioner and trainers' training in NLP

Distance Learning

You can also take our coaching training by distance learning by DVD.

We also sell individual DVDs on coaching, goals, values and beliefs. See our website for details.

To contact Lambent do Brasil, visit our website: www.lambentdobrasil.com
e-mail: info@lambentdobrasil.com

To find out more about the International Coaching Community, visit our website and contact: admin@lambentdobrasil.com

ABOUT THE AUTHORS

Joseph O'Connor

Joseph O'Connor is one of the best-known and respected trainers of NLP and coaching in the world. He has taught in North and South America, Hong Kong and Singapore (where he was awarded the medal of the National Community Leadership Institute), New Zealand and many European countries.

Joseph has worked with many companies as a trainer and a consultant, including BA, HP Invent and the United Nations Industrial Development Organization (UNIDO) in Vienna, consulting on industrial co-operation projects in developing countries.

He is the author of seventeen books, translated into twenty-one languages, including many of the best-selling and most respected books on NLP and communication skills. His book *Introducing NLP* has been used for over twelve years as the basic reference book for NLP study and has sold over 100,000 copies.

Joseph is co-founder of Lambent do Brasil. He lived in the UK for many years and now lives in Brazil.

Contact Joseph at joseph@lambentdobrasil.com

Andrea Lages

Andrea Lages is one of the most respected coaching trainers worldwide and a certified NLP trainer. She is the CEO and co-founder of Lambent do Brasil.

Living in São Paulo, Brazil, she works internationally as executive coach and business trainer doing courses and seminars on coaching, communication skills, systemic thinking, leadership and goal-setting with individuals and teams, and also training NLP trainers.

Andrea is fluent in English, Spanish and Portuguese and gives coaching and NLP courses in all the three languages.

She has worked in many different places in North and South America and many European countries.

Through her consultancy, Andrea designs and runs management development, training, coaching, customer services, team building, NLP application and systemic thinking in practical ways within organizations.

Contact Andrea at andrea@lambentdobrasil.com.

INDEX